DONNA
DE VARONA'S
HYDRO–
AEROBICS

DONNA DE VARONA'S HYDRO-AEROBICS

DONNA DE VARONA

and Barry Tarshis

Fawcett Columbine • New York

A Fawcett Columbine Book

Published by Ballantine Books

Library of Congress Catalog Card Number: 85-90891

ISBN: 0-449-90170-X

This edition published by arrangement with Macmillan Publishing Company

Manufactured in the United States of America

First Ballantine Books Trade Edition: March 1986

10 9 8 7 6 5 4 3 2 1

The ideas and instructions presented in this book are not intended as a substitute for consulting a physician. The reader should seek medical supervision before undertaking any exercise program.

With much love, I dedicate this book to my family, who has always supported me in whatever endeavor I decided to undertake. And because they are always there for me, I am encouraged to continue.

A special thanks to the thousands of coaches in this country who, with very little recognition or financial remuneration, help mold lives through their leadership in the competitive sport experience.

My thanks also to Frank McGuigan, my first coach, who recognized that although I had good toes for a developing diver, I was short on courage when it came to the high dives, and supported my change to competitive swimming. George Haines, who, through the years, has nurtured the skills of more women swimming champions than any other coach in history and helped me realize my potential. Bob Horn, UCLA Swimming and Water Polo coach, who so graciously gave of his time to help me with this project. Barry Tarshis, who is now ready to join the Master's Swimming Program after learning all the exercises in order to help write this book.

And finally, to all my special friends—in and out of sports—who recognize that for me, sports has been an important catalyst in learning how to compete in the biggest arena of all—life's arena!

CONTENTS

INTRODUCTION

I can guess what you're thinking: Does the world really need yet another book about physical fitness?

It's a good question, and let me answer by saying that hydro-aerobics represents an approach to physical fitness that is much different from the approach taken by other books on the subject with which you may be familiar. For what I've done in this book is to take one of the oldest, most popular and most universal activities known to the human race—swimming—and build around it a physical fitness program that will not only do what other fitness programs do (help you look better and feel better) but will enable you to achieve this level of fitness safely and enjoyably.

I'm committed to this program. I follow it myself and I'm convinced that it's the best program of its kind ever developed, although I have to admit that I'm hardly an objective observer. Indeed, when it comes to fitness and swimming, it is all but impossible for me to be objective. You might as well ask Billie Jean King to be objective about tennis, Pete Rose to be objective about baseball, or an opera freak to be objective about Pavarotti.

Then again, it's always been that way with me for as long as I can remember. Swimming and fitness were passions of mine long before I began preparing for the Olympics, and they have remained passions long since I retired from competitive swimming at the over-the-hill age of seventeen. Some athletes lose interest in their sport once they stop competing, but my interest in—and my love for—swimming is as intense today as it's ever been. I work out in the water *all the time*: whenever I'm home in New York and whenever I travel, which I do at least twelve months a year. (My swimsuit, in fact, is the first thing I pack.) Make that swim*suits*: one for my suitcase and one for my purse. You never know.

I work out in the water for any number of different reasons, but mostly I do it to keep fit—physically fit and mentally fit. I work out in the water to control my weight (a constant battle), to meditate (often about why I have trouble controlling my weight), to solve problems, and to get away from the stresses and tensions that pop in and out of my life almost daily.

Mostly, though, I work out in the water because I love it. No matter how busy or preoccupied I might be with my career or whatever might be going on in my personal or professional life, I know I can always count on swimming. There's something very special—and I'm not sure I understand it—between water and me, something almost mystical. There is a feeling I get when I'm working out in the water that I get no place else. It's not a feeling I can describe, or one I would even choose to describe; it's that personal. It's a feeling, on the other hand, that will always be important to me. It's part of who I am as a person.

I don't think I'm alone in this feeling. In fact, the latest statistics on recreation in the United States suggest that swimming may well be the single most popular sporting activity in this country. Something like 100 million Americans know how to swim and report that they enjoy the activity, and nearly 30 million Americans, according to the latest numbers, swim (during warm weather, at least) several times a week. The Red Cross alone, over the past seven decades, has awarded more than 60 million certificates for swimming and 5 million for lifesaving. And the number of in-ground pools in the United States, which is now more than 2 million, has more than tripled in only the past two decades.

That's the good news. The not-so-good news, as far as I'm concerned, is that for every serious swimmer—and I'm using the term "serious" here to describe anyone who works out in the water at least two times a week—there are probably a hundred who swim only now and then and do not begin to derive the benefits and enjoyment that swimming has the potential to give.

And even among serious swimmers, as far as I have been able to see, it's harder than you might think to find people who are taking *full* advantage of everything swimming has to offer.

What I'm saying here is that despite the tens of millions of people who swim regularly, swimming, to my mind, is still an undiscovered sport—a sport whose pleasures and benefits are largely unknown to most people.

There are several reasons that swimming is an undeniably popular sport today and yet a sport whose potential has only begun to be tapped, and I'll touch upon some of the reasons a little later in the book. For now, though, let me say simply that most people who work out in the water shortchange themselves in one of two ways: One, they do not swim properly, which is to say that they swim in a manner that runs counter to the basic mechanical principles of the sport. (And let me put in quickly here that it's not much harder—it's easier, in fact, in most cases— to swim properly. That's one of the many wonderful things about swimming.) And two, there is an attitude among many swimmers—particularly among swimmers who rely on the sport for fitness—that if you use swimming to keep fit, you need to be something of a Spartan; that it's a sport in which you have little choice but to suffer, to make sacrifices, and to go through workouts that are repetitious and boring.

I hope to prove to you in this book that the "sacrifices" you have to make in order to build a fitness program around swimming are minimal compared to the benefits and the sheer joy a Hydro-Aerobics workout will bring you. I hope to prove to you that the Hydro-Aerobics program you'll learn about in this book can be not only healthy but fun and invigorating and, above all, interesting. I hope to prove to you that you will look forward to your Hydro-Aerobics workouts the way I look forward to mine— with the same enthusiasm and excitement that you might have had toward swimming when you were much younger. Come to think of it, that might well be one of the most appealing benefits of Hydro-Aerobics—that simply being in the water brings out the child in us, assuming, that is, that we approach it in the right manner and with the right attitude. As my good friend and longtime mentor Bob Horn, the swimming coach of UCLA, likes to put it, "The thing I stress more than any other about swimming isn't that it's an excellent fitness activity and a terrific way to reduce tension. The thing I stress over and over again is that swimming should be, above all, a pleasant experience. It should be fun."

Not only *should* but *can*. And here, I think, is where this book may differ from other books on swimming or from books on other fitness programs. For more than simply spelling out the specifics of a total fitness program, this book will show you how to incorporate Hydro-Aerobics into your life in the most enjoyable way possible, so that your workouts become a regular part of your life—not because you *have* to do them in order to keep fit but because you genuinely look forward to them and because the workouts leave you with a sense of vitality, of accomplishment, and of joy. I'm tired of hearing people apologize for swimming and for keeping fit, and tired of hearing all the reasons people *don't* swim. One of my prime objectives of this book, in other words, is to change the way you think about fitness and swimming—and, in the process, perhaps to change your life as well.

DONNA DE VARONA'S HYDRO-AEROBICS

1· The Many "Whys" of Swimming

One morning a few months ago I found myself in the middle of a lively conversation at an indoor swim club. Except for me, everybody else at the club was a member, and the subject of the conversation was why each of the persons who worked out at the club did so.

One of the regulars was an insurance executive in his late fifties, who said he worked out in the water because he'd had a heart attack two years before and had been urged by his doctor to take up swimming. Another regular was an airline pilot who had begun to swim for fitness a year or two before, following an operation on a knee he'd hurt playing tennis, and who had stuck with swimming even after the knee had healed because he found swimming a lot less frustrating than tennis. There were two women in their mid- to late thirties, who told me they swam to keep fit and to keep their weight down. There was a stockbroker in her late twenties who told me she swam because it was one of few things she did that was totally relaxing for her; a woman who admitted that one of the main reasons she swam was that she enjoyed the camaraderie of the group; and three or four men and women who couldn't articulate any specific reason for swimming other than the fact that they enjoyed doing it.

This diversity of answers didn't surprise me, nor should it you. The fact is, anytime you assemble a group of swimmers and ask them why they swim, you can expect the same diversity. And that's one of the great features of swimming—it can deliver benefits and pleasures on so many different levels.

3

I'm aware, of course, that swimming isn't the only sport that has this quality. Runners, tennis players, golfers—get any group of athletes in a particular sport to talk about their reasons for participating, and you're going to find the same diversity of motivation.

But at the risk of offending those of you who are partial to a sport other than swimming, I don't know of any that offers quite as *much* as swimming and can appeal to so many different people in so many different age groups in so many different ways. So, before we get into the specifics of my Hydro-Aerobics program, let's look briefly at why the water holds so much appeal for so many different kinds of people.

Swimming as a Fitness Activity

Enough has been written of late about the benefits of getting into good physical shape—both the long-term benefits of better health and the short-term benefits of simply feeling good—that I'm going to spare you the usual lecture on how fitness can change your life. You know—or you *should* know, at any rate—that when you are physically fit, you look better, you feel better, you sleep better, you work more efficiently and you are far less susceptible to certain life-style ailments such as high blood pressure, nervous tension, and, according to the latest research, diabetes and heart disease.

What you may not have heard, however, is the degree to which working out in the *water* can contribute to your fitness. For whatever else exercise physiologists may disagree about—and there's plenty of disagreement to go around in the new and rapidly growing field of exercise science—nearly everyone would agree that no sport is a better all-around activity than swimming.

Notice I said "all around." *Total* fitness is usually talked about in three basic categories: (1) cardiovascular, or aerobic, fitness, which involves the ability of your heart and lungs to transport blood and oxygen to your muscles; (2) flexibility, which has to do with how much range of motion there is in the various joints throughout your body; and (3) muscular strength and endurance,

How Swimming Stacks Up against Other Sports

Several years ago, the President's Council on Physical Fitness and Sports asked a panel of seven medical and fitness experts to rate 14 sports on a scale of 0–3 in each of the categories below, plus one other category (balance) not listed. A perfect score from this panel would have been 21. Here are the results.

Sport	Stamina	Muscular Endurance	Strength	Flexibility	Total
Swimming	21	20	14	15	**70**
Handball/Squash	19	18	15	16	**68**
Jogging	21	20	17	9	**67**
Skiing—cross country	19	19	15	14	**67**
Basketball	19	17	15	13	**64**
Skiing—downhill	16	18	15	14	**63**
Skating—ice or roller	18	17	15	13	**63**
Bicycling	19	18	16	9	**62**
Tennis	16	16	14	14	**60**
Calisthenics	10	13	16	19	**58**
Walking	13	14	11	7	**45**
Golf	8	8	9	8	**33**
Softball	6	8	7	9	**30**
Bowling	5	5	5	7	**22**

Source: The President's Council on Physical Fitness and Sports

which has to do with how much force your muscles are capable of generating and for how long a period.

As it happens, most sports and fitness activities deliver benefits in only one or at the most two of these activities. Running, for instance, is an excellent aerobic conditioner, but it does almost nothing for your flexibility (if anything, running tends to tighten muscles) and little to tone muscles other than those in your legs. Calisthenics and stretching exercises like yoga are good for flexibility but not particularly good for strength and only marginally beneficial to your heart and lungs. The ball sports, like tennis and racquetball, are good for flexibility but do little for muscle strength and require a fairly intense participation level in order to produce aerobic benefits. Weight training and programs using machines such as the Nautilus are good for building strength and increasing flexibility, but you have to go through the routines very quickly to gain any real cardiovascular benefits from them.

Swimming: Is It the Perfect Exercise?

Which brings us to swimming. I don't think I'd go as far as some people who've described swimming as the perfect exercise ("perfect," after all, is a word I've heard used to define at least a half-dozen fitness activities that range from jumping rope to weight training). But swimming, it's fair to say, comes closer to perfection than any other sport or exercise program I can think of. I don't hesitate to say this because swimming is better than any *one* fitness activity at producing benefits in each of the three major fitness areas. Swimming forces the heart and lungs to pump oxygen to all the major muscle groups throughout the body, and as a result, is as aerobically beneficial as running, cycling, or cross-country skiing. Swimming involves the long stretching movements you use routinely in calisthenics, and as a result, is an excellent means of developing and maintaining flexibility. And because swimming obliges you to make these movements against the natural resistance of the water, it enhances the tone and strength of your muscles.

But the beauty of swimming goes beyond its ability to deliver a variety of fitness benefits. Equally important is the fact that swimming is a fitness activity with a very low injury factor—so low that one of the first things professional athletes recovering from injuries are instructed to do is to swim. Ankle sprains, tender elbows, sore backs, blisters, stress fractures, tendonitis—all the workaday aches and pains that plague weekend athletes who jog, play tennis, or lift weights are virtually unheard of among people who work out in the water. Sure, once in a while, if you overdo it and if you're not careful, you can pull a muscle when you swim, and swimmers probably have a higher incidence of sinus problems than most people, but most regular swimmers can go for years and years without even a minor injury.

Water: Gentle Resistance

What makes swimming so low an injury-risk sport, of course, is the nature of water itself. Unlike pavement, wood, or even dirt, water doesn't increase the effects of gravity; it reduces these effects. The water offers resistance—an important principle in exercise—but it's gentle, *passive* resistance. Water gives; it doesn't jolt. And as a result, you do not punish your joints when you swim the same way you punish them in other sports. Water also keeps your muscles relaxed and loose (as long as the water isn't too cold) and it stimulates circulation, which means that more of your muscles get oxygen and you achieve a broader range of motion than in other sports.

These characteristics of water explain why people who have leg or knee injuries or suffer from arthritis can still enjoy the benefits of fitness through swimming. I don't know if you're aware of it, but swimming has extended the careers of more than a few professional athletes, for example, Joe Namath. Each time he had to recuperate from knee surgery, Namath followed a carefully regimented swimming program, and the last I heard, he was still swimming regularly. One of the first exercises many athletes recovering from serious knee injuries do is simply to *walk* in a swimming pool. The reason is that the gentle resistance of the water strengthens the muscles without risking added injury to the knee.

No need to belabor the obvious. As I'll point out in the next chapter, the fact that swimming has so low an injury risk is one of the chief reasons that aerobics experts such as Dr. Kenneth Cooper rank swimming so high as a regular aerobics activity. After all, it's difficult to stay fit if the very activity you're relying on for fitness has a tendency to put you out of commission for days and even weeks at a time.

Swimming to Control Your Weight

If you are overweight and you were to begin a Hydro-Aerobics program tomorrow, you could probably lose a good fifteen to twenty pounds within three months—*and not have to reduce your food intake.*

There's no mystery here. Controlling weight is mainly a matter of burning more calories than you take in, and nothing is better at burning calories than exercise—especially a vigorous exercise like swimming. Swimming, however, is possibly the only fitness activity in which being overweight is actually something of an advantage.

What do I mean by "advantage?" Well, for starters, any extra fat cells you might be carrying around serve as an insulator and keep you a little warmer than you would be if you didn't have them. (Am I stretching here? Maybe so, but heck, when you're a little overweight in our society—and I can tell you this from personal experience—you need all the moral support you can get.)

But a more compelling reason that a Hydro-Aerobics program makes so much sense for people who are overweight is that any extra pounds you're carrying give your body added buoyancy, which means that you float more easily and you encounter less resistance in the water than somebody who is a lot thinner. In other words, swimming, and in particular, most of the Hydro-Aerobics exercises we'll be working with, is generally easier for people who are overweight (everything else being equal) than for people who are thin.

So if you are uncomfortably—and unhealthily—overweight and looking for a regular fitness activity to burn off excess calories, Hydro-Aerobics will spare you much of the pain and the awkwardness that you might otherwise have to experience if you were trying to burn off those calories in, say, an exercise class or on a tennis court. You don't have to worry about feeling awkward when you swim, and as a result, you're much more likely to *stay* with swimming as a regular fitness activity than you would these other sports. I have a theory—and it's only a theory—that if more people who were overweight knew how pleasant and enjoyable exercise can be in the water, there would be fewer people with serious weight problems.

Extra Fringes for the Overweight

Logic would seem to indicate that the more you exercise, the more you want to eat, but most people who exercise regularly— myself included—find that you tend to eat *less*, not more, after a workout.

There's a biological basis for this phenomenon, and it has to do with the fact that once you've gotten into a regular exercise routine, your blood sugar level remains relatively stable. But there's a psychological dynamic at work here as well. Vigorous

---

How much do you really know about calories?

One of the keys to controlling your weight is being aware of the calories in the foods you eat most frequently. Here's a little true or false quiz to test your calories I.Q. The answers (page 11) may surprise you.

1. Margarine has fewer calories than butter.
2. A dish of ice cream has more calories than a hamburger.
3. Almonds have more calories than peanuts.
4. The yolk of the egg has more calories than the white of the egg.
5. Cheesecake has more calories than a lamb chop.
6. A Big Mac has more calories than 3 pieces of Kentucky Fried Chicken.
7. Wine has fewer calories than beer.
8. White flour has fewer calories than whole wheat flour.
9. Italian bread has fewer calories than pumpernickel bread.
10. A pancake has fewer calories than a piece of white bread.

---

exercise, whether it's swimming or running or whatever, tends to reduce the stresses and tensions that increase appetite and, in so doing, reduces the *need* to binge. I tend to eat the most when I'm the busiest and under the most pressure, and that's why the busier and more pressured I am, the more disciplined I am about my workouts. I know that if I can exercise for even a half-hour during, say, lunchtime, that I'll eat less than I normally would when the time comes to sit down to a meal.

For the record, and there are all kinds of variables here, the Hydro-Aerobics workouts I'll be describing for you in this book will burn up between 200 and 350 calories an hour, depending, of course, on how vigorously you swim and depending, too, on your own body composition. And if you know how many calories are in some of your favorite foods, you can motivate yourself the way I do. "Well," I'll sometimes think to myself after I've worked out in the water for about fifteen minutes, "now I've earned the right to have an extra beer or, if I really work hard, maybe a sundae for dessert."

I'm aware that if you're overweight, you might be self-conscious about the way you look in a bathing suit. But look at it this way: Once you overcome that initial self-consciousness, you'll have an added measure of motivation: the desire to look better and better in a bathing suit each time you work out.

Don't laugh. I have a friend whose system of dieting is based on that very principle. About a month before she intends to go on vacation, she buys a very brief bikini, and whenever she is tempted over the next few weeks to miss an exercise workout or to eat something fattening, she thinks of herself in the bikini and is able to summon all the self-discipline she needs.

While I'm on the subject of how you look in a bathing suit, let me interject a personal observation. I have long since accepted the fact that I'll never look like Christie Brinkley or Cheryl Tiegs in a bathing suit, and so I don't expect miracles from swimming. Like most women I know, there are times when I would like to shed a few pounds, but I value how I *feel* more than how I *look*, and I know that it isn't weight alone that determines the figure you show to the rest of the world; it's the way your body is composed and the way you carry yourself. In fact, whenever my weight drops below normal, people don't tell me how good I look; they want to know if I'm feeling well.

But I can tell you this: Once you get involved with Hydro-Aerobics on a regular basis, you'll start seeing a big difference in the makeup of your body—and for an easily explained reason. When you exercise—and, in particular, when you do the kind of exercises you'll be doing with Hydro-Aerobics—your body will start to burn the fat that is stored in the usual places the body stores fat: in the stomach, thighs, hips, and buttocks. This is particularly important if you're a woman, because women, remember, have a higher percentage of body fat than men to begin with—about 25 percent, as compared to 15 percent for men—and for this reason have to work harder to keep supple.

Answers:

1. **False.** Margarine and butter have the same number of calories: about 100 per tablespoon.
2. **False.** A hamburger (without the bun) has about 225 calories, while an average portion of ice cream has only about 100.
3. **True.** Most nuts are high in calories but almonds (213 per handful) have more than peanuts (185).
4. **True.** The yolk of an egg (60 calories) is four times as fattening as the white of the egg.
5. **False.** A piece of cheesecake and a lamb chop have the same number of calories.
6. **False.** The Colonel wins by a nose: 660 calories for the 3-piece special to 557 for the Big Mac.
7. **False.** An eight-ounce glass of beer has only 100 calories. The equivalent amount of wine would be nearly 200 calories.
8. **False.** Both white and whole wheat flour have the same number of calories—about 400 per cup.
9. **True.** Italian bread has 55 calories while pumpernickel has about 85.
10. **True.** A pancake has about 60 calories. A piece of enriched white bread has 65.

Swimming as a Form of Meditation

Several years ago, when I went on a speaker's tour for *Sports Illustrated*, the one thing I insisted upon was that the Speaker's Bureau of the magazine contact the sponsors in each of the cities in which I was appearing and make arrangements for me to swim there, so that I wouldn't have to beg for a place to swim.

I wasn't being difficult; I simply know myself. I know that apart from everything else, swimming is an important orienting and centering device for me. Wherever I am or however busy I am, swimming restores my mental equilibrium. It is literally my home away from home.

On that tour, for instance, I often used swimming workouts as a time to evaluate my last speech and to think about things I might do to make the next speech that much more effective.

I've always been aware of this aspect of swimming, but I never realized the extent to which I rely on it until early 1980, when I was covering the Olympics boycott story for NBC Sports. I had just flown back from Moscow with an exclusive interview, and no sooner had I landed in New York than the network asked me to fly to Munich that night, do five interviews back to back, and then fly home the next day and go to Washington.

Those few days may well have been the busiest—certainly the most pressure filled—of my life other than my Olympics competition days, and if you asked me what got me through them, I can answer without any hesitation. At six o'clock in the morning on the day following the interviews in Munich, as tired as I was and as punchy as I was, I forced myself to get up and went through a forty-five-minute workout in the pool of the Munich Hilton, a hotel I'd deliberately chosen because it not only has a nice pool but it is also kept open twenty-four hours a day.

Water as the Ultimate Security Blanket

I could tell you dozens of stories like the one I've just related, as could most serious swimmers. Runners, I know, will often tell you the same thing: the half-hour or so they spend running helps clear their minds and puts them into a productive mental groove. I don't question the ability of running to do this, but I don't think that running is as dependable a mental relaxant as swimming. Nor can any of the more competitive fitness activities—tennis and racquetball, for instance—relax you mentally as much as swimming does. I enjoy running and I like to play tennis, but when I'm running along the road I'm so wary of traffic (not to mention dogs) that I can't really relax, and when I'm competing against somebody on the other side of the net, I'm as likely to be frustrated after it's over as I am to be relaxed. When I'm doing my workouts in the water, I have neither of these concerns.

If you swim regularly, of course, you probably know what I'm talking about, but chances are good that you find it hard to explain just what it is about the water that is able to produce such peace of mind. I've had psychologists tell me that being in the water takes us back to our prenatal beginnings and thus represents in some respects the ultimate feeling of security. I don't know how much I subscribe to this theory, but I do know, as I mentioned in the Introduction, that swimming is unique in its ability to make me feel comfortable and secure.

Swimming to Broaden Your Life

There are certainly worse problems to have in life, I suppose, but I genuinely feel sorry for people who shy away from the water because they have never learned to swim properly. Why? Because once you've developed some basic swimming skills, there is an excitingly varied world of water-based activities that you can incorporate into your life. You can enjoy sailing or snorkeling and, if you take the time to learn it, you can scuba dive. If you're younger, you can get involved with surfing, with sail boarding (definitely a sport of the future) or with waterskiing.

Each of these different sports, apart from being a lot of fun, adds a new dimension to your leisure life. Each can open up more vacation options and, at the same time, help you meet new people and make new friends. And, incidentally, you don't have to be a strong swimmer to enjoy these activities or, for that matter, to take part in the Hydro-Aerobics routines I'll be describing for you later in the book. What's more, regardless of

Eight Myths about Swimming and Fitness

1. Swimming too much will make you muscle-bound.

This myth probably got started because a lot of muscle-bound people like to go to the beach or a pool to show off their bodies. Chances are good that some of these people never even swim. If they did, their muscles would be elongated and smooth, not bulky, for this is what swimming does for your muscles.

2. No pain, no gain.

The notion that you can only become fit by suffering exhaustion and waking up the next morning stiff and achy is so deeply entrenched, I'm hesitant to question it lest I be branded an athletic heretic. The plain truth, however, is that if you plan your workouts intelligently, you will never reach a point of total exhaustion—only a feeling of exuberance and well-being. And your progress will be every bit as rapid and steady as someone who is determined to suffer.

3. The colder the water, the better it is for you.

I have no idea how this myth got started (perhaps it was somebody with a polar bear complex), but it has yet to be proved that except for comfort, the temperature of the water makes any difference in how much you get from a workout. If anything, very cold water can be dangerous if you jump right into it: The shock to your body could, under some circumstances, cause a heart attack.

4. Swimmers are more apt to get colds than other people.

Swimmers with sensitive nostrils and sinuses may well have runnier noses after they've finished swimming than other people, and if you're not careful about dressing warmly after swimming on a cold day, you could well catch more colds than other people. Otherwise, however, there is no evidence at all to support the notion that swimming itself can cause colds.

5. Swimming is bad for your skin and hair.

I can only speak for myself and for other swimmers I know, but I've yet to see any evidence that swimming is harmful to either skin or hair. Granted, some people are more sensitive to chlorine than others, and certain types of hair—hair that's been chemically treated or is difficult to manage to begin with—are a little more difficult to manage if you swim. But as long as you take the time to rinse or shampoo your hair each time you swim, you shouldn't run into problems.

6. You need to work out every day in order to get anything out of swimming.

If you're aiming for the Olympics, maybe, but if you're looking for a level of fitness that will give you that wonderful feeling of energy and well-being day in and day out, you don't have to work out more than three days a week and you can spend as little as forty-five minutes a day (even less, if you want to concentrate on aerobic fitness alone) and still gain an enormous amount of benefit from the sport.

7. Swimming is boring.

To some people, maybe—but not if you take full advantage of all the variety that swimming has to offer, which is exactly what my Hydro-Aerobics program enables you to do.

8. Swimming interferes with other sports.

This may be the biggest myth of all about swimming, particularly since the opposite happens to be true. If you run regularly, swimming will increase your flexibility and greatly reduce your chances of injury while you're running. If you play tennis, squash, or racquetball, swimming will help increase your stamina. In fact, far from interfering with your ability to perform, the proper swimming program would actually improve your performance in any sport.

your age or how you feel about the water, you're never too old to learn to swim. It may interest you to learn, for instance, that before he starred in the movie *The Swimmer*, Burt Lancaster, who is a superb athlete, not only didn't know how to swim but was actually afraid of the water. But Burt worked with Bob Horn, who has taught any number of celebrities how to swim, and has gone on to become a very strong swimmer.

Hydro-Aerobics: A Lifetime Fitness Activity

Reaping the long-term benefits of any athletic or fitness activity has a lot to do with how easy—or how difficult—it is to incorporate that activity into your life-style, regardless of your age and where you happen to live. And I can think of no fitness program that scores higher in this regard than Hydro- Aerobics.

Swimming itself is a sport a child takes up almost as soon as he or she has learned how to walk, and it's a sport that, as long as you're basically healthy, you're never too old to take part in. I've run into people in their eighties who swim every day and who, in fact, attribute their longevity and health to their swimming.

Hydro-Aerobics is probably not quite as convenient a fitness activity for most people as running. After all, you can run just about anywhere (weather permitting), do it alone or with others, and do it with a bare minimum of equipment.

Hydro-Aerobics isn't that far behind. No matter where you live chances are good that there is a pool not far from your home or your place of work. It may be in a Y, a swim club, a school, a community center, an apartment complex, a park, a friend's home, or a hotel. And I don't care how much you travel, either, or where you travel to; you can almost always incorporate Hydro-Aerobics into your schedule. Many of the newer hotels today have their own pools, and most top hotels that don't have a pool do have affiliations with nearby clubs, so that if you want to swim, they can arrange it for you.

I speak from personal experience. I travel much more than most people, yet I have rarely found myself in a situation in which I simply couldn't find a place to work out in the water. Normally I try to stay at a hotel that has a pool on the premises, but I've made other arrangements when the need has arisen.

When I was in Helsinki during the 1983 World Championships of Track and Field, I worked out in the Baltic Sea and enjoyed every moment of it. On trips to Canada I've done my workouts in lakes. And on the few occasions on which I have traveled to Moscow, I've worked out in the Moscow public pool, which, incidentally, is the largest indoor pool in the world.

What's particularly convenient about swimming, of course, is the fact that once you've found a pool or lake, you don't need any special equipment. I should point out quickly that I do recommend certain swimming aids—goggles, for example, and fins—to help you get more out of your Hydro-Aerobics workouts, but none of this equipment is absolutely essential. Other than a bathing suit (and even that, in certain situations, isn't a necessity), all you need to take with you into the water for a Hydro-Aerobics workout is *you*.

Summing Up the Benefits

I could probably go on singing the praises of swimming for pages and pages, but by now I think you've begun to get my drift. So to close this chapter, let me simply repeat some of the key benefits of this sport that I am so partial to:

- Swimming improves your fitness level in the three major categories: cardiovascular conditioning, flexibility, and strength.
- Swimming produces this improvement with a very low injury factor.
- Swimming improves your appearance by helping you maintain your weight and by adding a strong measure of grace to your movements.
- Swimming is refreshing: You finish your workouts feeling energetic and renewed.
- Swimming is relaxing: It's one of the few forms of exercise in which the environment—the water—is relaxing in and of itself.
- Swimming is convenient: It's something you can do year-round, at home or when you travel.
- Swimming is fun: It gives you the opportunity to develop a skill (at your own pace) and see steady improvement.

2· HYDRO-AEROBICS: WHAT IT CAN DO FOR YOU

For most people who swim, working out is mainly a matter of swimming laps. The distance may vary and so may the speed of the lap and the strokes you do, but the basic format of the workout is usually the same: You swim from one end of the pool to the other or around the pool in a circle.

Not that I'm knocking the practice of swimming laps. Far from it. If you did nothing but swim laps for twenty to thirty minutes a day three days a week, you would be in terrific shape.

But workouts that consist almost entirely of lap swimming have certain limitations. First of all, the repetitious nature of lap swimming, even if you vary the strokes, is something that many people—myself included—find tedious and monotonous, and I know more than a few people who've quit swimming for this very reason: They found lap swimming too dull.

Another problem with lap swimming is that you're exercising only those muscles involved in a particular stroke. True, regardless of what stroke you're doing, you involve more muscles than you would doing other fitness activities. But even if you swam every day and varied your strokes each day—crawl one day, breaststroke the next, and so on—certain muscle groups would not get enough of a workout to achieve a truly balanced fitness. In particular, you wouldn't be building any true measure of strength in your muscles.

Hydro-Aerobics is different. It delivers the same aerobic benefits as lap swimming but offers more variety and more interest, and it delivers a broader range of fitness. What it does is combine lap swimming with basic elements of calisthenics, stretching, and

19

strength-building training to produce benefits not only in each of the three major fitness areas—cardiovascular fitness, flexibility and strength—but is varied enough to avoid the boredom that is so often the case with lap swimming.

The Workouts in Brief

Each of the Hydro-Aerobics workouts I've set up for you in this book is just that—a workout. The program emphasizes what most exercise experts consider the most important of the three fitness categories—aerobic fitness—but it combines aerobic swimming with stretching movements, water calisthenics, and strength-building exercises.

Let's look more closely now at some of the specific features of these workouts:

• **Balance.** Each of the workouts listed later in the book gives you the opportunity, in one session, to improve your cardio-vascular conditioning, your flexibility, and your strength. What's more, you will have the option (and I'll explain later how to use this option) to expand or reduce the amount of time you spend on each of these categories to meet your particular fitness goals.

• **Simplicity.** I've done my best to keep both the workouts and the individual routines as simple as possible. As you'll see, some of the routines call for special equipment, such as kickboards or strength-building devices known as floaties. Using these special swimming aids is advisable but not essential. You'll have optional exercises that call for no special equipment at all.

• **Variety.** I've deliberately put together a number of different workouts for each of the various levels of fitness and swimming ability into which the program is divided. I've done this mainly to make the program on the whole more interesting for you. You can vary these programs in any number of ways. You might choose to do the same workout each day you swim during a single week, or you might want to vary workouts daily.

Hydro-Aerobics: The Basic Elements

The specific elements of each Hydro-Aerobics workout fall into six different but intermingled segments: warm-up, bobbing, lap swimming, flexibility exercises, strength exercises, and cool-down. Let's look briefly at each.

The Warm-up and Cool-down

The warm-up segment of a Hydro-Aerobics workout has two parts. The first is a set of simple stretching exercises that you can do either out of or in the water, depending on your preference. The second is a brief segment of either relaxed swimming or bobbing, the purpose of which is to increase your heart rate and to get your body primed for the actual workout.

The cool-down segment comes at the end of each workout and consists of a few minutes of stretching designed to loosen whatever muscles may have tightened during the workout and to give your pulse a chance to slow down.

Bobbing

Bobbing is a basic water exercise that novice swimmers do to develop the proper breathing habits for swimming, but it's an excellent water exercise, too, for advanced swimmers. That's why I've made it part of every Hydro-Aerobics workout.

Bobbing serves several basic functions in Hydro-Aerobics: first, it sets into motion a healthy breathing pattern that contributes to your aerobic fitness; second, it relaxes you; and finally, it's simply exhilarating.

Lap Swimming

There are two kinds of lap swimming in Hydro-Aerobics: sprint swimming, in which you swim as fast as you can for short periods, and aerobic swimming, in which the objective is to get your heart beating at a certain target level for a long enough time to produce what fitness specialists like to call the aerobic training effect. (See pp. 134 to 136 for a complete discussion of target pulse rate and training effect.)

The bulk of the lap or sprint swimming in your Hydro-Aerobics workouts will be done using the crawl, because that stroke is the most basic of the four strokes and, all things considered, delivers the best ratio of effort to cardiovascular benefit. In certain instances, however, you'll have an option and thus will have the opportunity, too, to develop your proficiency in other strokes as well and to develop those muscles involved with other strokes.

Flexibility Exercises

These exercises (some people call them hydro-calisthenics) are designed to give greater elasticity to specific muscle groups, particularly those muscle groups that control movement in the major joints in the body: the hips, the knees, and the shoulders. The more flexible you are, the more fluid and graceful you are in your movements and the easier it is for you to get in and out of a car smoothly and, as you get older, to do basic things like bend to tie your shoes.

Most of the flexibility exercises in Hydro-Aerobics will involve the larger and more important muscle groups in the body: the muscles in your legs and thighs, your abdomen, your back, and your arms and shoulders. But you won't have to spend too much time in each workout doing these exercises. The combination of the exercises themselves and doing them in the water will give more than enough flexibility.

Strength Exercises

The basic idea behind strength-development exercises is a principle known as *overload*. You simply work a muscle harder, longer or more frequently than it is accustomed to working, with the idea that ultimately the muscle will undergo physiological changes to adapt to the increased load. Swimming in and of itself produces a certain amount of overload, because the natural resistance of the water forces your muscles to work harder than normally, but swimming, as I mentioned in the first chapter, isn't as effective a strength builder as weight training or using Nautilus machines. Still, there are specific exercises—and specific devices, such as "floaties"—that use this resistance factor more effectively. The strength exercises you'll be doing in Hydro-Aerobics are not designed to build your muscles as much as they are to give your muscles more tone.

Hydro-Aerobics and the Chemistry of Exercise

Hydro-aerobics is built around a number of basic exercise concepts that relate to what happens chemically when you work out, and I think it's a good idea to understand something about these chemical dynamics. The more you know about fitness, the more intelligent you can be in your approach to your own fitness program.

Let's start with the basics. No muscle movement can take place unless there is energy to fuel it, and all the muscle cells in our body contain a substance known as adenosine triphosphate (ATP) that is able to "burn" nutrients and in this way supply the fuel that each cell needs to carry on its biological business.

Also present in the cell is a chemical compound called creatine phosphate (CP), whose principal function is to keep the cell supplied with ATP. Together these two chemical substances constitute a form of energy known as the ATP-CP, or the phosphate energy system. It's a powerful system, all things considered, but it gets burned very quickly during intense activity. If you were to try to run or swim as fast as you could, the ATP-CP system would be out of fuel within ten seconds.

Anaerobic and Aerobic Energy

The energy supplied by the ATP-CP system is generally referred to as *anaerobic* (without air) energy, but it is not the only source of such energy. Our muscle cells can also tap a form of energy that has its source in lactic acid, a substance that originates in certain foods we eat—carbohydrates, mainly—and is stored in the liver until it is needed by muscle cells and then gets converted to a fuel known as glycogen.

In most people, these two anaerobic energy systems—the phosphates and lactic acid—can support intense energy for approximately a minute and a half. What happens after this anaerobic supply is gone and you want to maintain activity? Nothing mysterious. The muscle cells involved in this intense activity

must now rely on an outside source of energy, namely oxygen, to refuel the chemical machinery that underlies the production of fuel in each cell. And here is where *aerobic* (with air) energy enters the picture. No longer able to tap existing ATP-CP within its own domain and unable to make use of glycogen, muscle cells now rely on the heart, the lungs, and the vascular system to supply these cells with the oxygen needed to generate ATP.

Aerobic Fitness: A Closer Look

When we talk about aerobic fitness, we're talking essentially about the ability of the body's cardiovascular system to supply and transport oxygen in sufficient amounts to muscles that have used up existing energy supplies but are still engaged in heavy work. As long as the supply keeps pace with the demand, work can go on, but when the demand exceeds supply, the cells literally run out of fuel, and this produces the sensation—and often the pain—that we recognize as fatigue.

The person most responsible for our understanding of aerobic fitness is Dr. Kenneth Cooper, the well-known founder and director of the Aerobics Center in Dallas, Texas. Dr. Cooper defined aerobic exercise as any activity that requires oxygen for a prolonged enough period so that the body must improve its capacity to handle oxygen. His view—and it's a view that more and more physicians, exercise physiologists, and researchers have come to accept in recent years—is that aerobic exercise produces "beneficial changes" in the lungs, the heart, and the vascular system. "More specifically," says Dr. Cooper, "regular exercise of this type enhances the ability of the body to move air into and out of lungs; the total blood volume increases; and the blood becomes better equipped to transport oxygen."

The actual benefits that come from enhanced aerobic fitness used to be a great source of debate, but this is less so today. Some people still question whether aerobic fitness is a guarantee against having a heart attack, but it's generally agreed that aerobic fitness is one of the factors (along with diet, weight, stress, life-style, genetics, etc.) that figure in heart disease, and no one questions any longer that when you are aerobically fit, you simply *feel* better: You have more energy, you sleep better, you're less prone to colds and to digestive problems, and you deal with life in general with a greater sense of vitality and well-being.

Swimming and Aerobics

Dr. Cooper rates swimming as the second most effective exercise you can perform for aerobic fitness (the first, by the way, is cross-country skiing, according to Cooper's latest studies).

How did Cooper arrive at this position? Well, to measure the effectiveness of an aerobic exercise, Cooper uses two criteria: one, the degree to which the activity providing the exercise "forces the body to improve those systems responsible for the transportation of oxygen" (mainly the heart and lungs); and two, that the activity be interesting—and safe—enough so that you can continue with it for your entire lifetime.

Swimming scores very high on both counts. First of all, swimming involves all the major muscles in the body, which means that whenever you're swimming, you're forcing the heart and lungs to pump oxygen to more muscles and at a faster rate than they would be forced to do in an exercise involving fewer muscles. Second—and this is an aspect of swimming that even Kenneth Cooper doesn't talk that much about—swimming forces you to breathe efficiently, and in so doing, it enhances the aerobic benefits.

But just as important as what swimming does for your aerobic fitness is what swimming doesn't do to you—the fact that swimming, as I mentioned in the last chapter, provides its aerobic conditioning effect at a cost to your body that is far less punishing than is the case with other popular aerobic sports, in particular, running.

Please don't misunderstand. I know almost as many dedicated runners as I do dedicated swimmers. So I don't want to turn this discussion into a swimming-versus-running debate. But most people would agree, I think, that runners on the whole, as a group, pay a heavier price for aerobic conditioning when it comes to aches, pains, and minor injuries than swimmers do. And it's this difference between swimming and running, by the way, that accounts for why Dr. Cooper ranked swimming just ahead of running and jogging in his book *The Aerobics Program for Total Well-Being*.

Hydro-Aerobics and Your Swimming Ability

One of the best things about Hydro-Aerobics is that you do not have to be an especially strong swimmer to benefit from the workouts. At the same time, however, one of the goals of the program as a whole is to help you improve both your swimming endurance—how long you can swim—and your swimming technique—how smoothly you swim.

So even if you can't swim more than a few laps, you can still find a workout that will keep you active in the water for at least forty to forty-five minutes. Gradually, though, as you work out more often, you will be able to increase the amount of time you are able to swim without stopping, and you won't have to sacrifice other elements of your fitness while you are achieving these new plateaus.

3· THE HYDRO-AEROBICS EXERCISES

Now that you know something about the logic of the Hydro-Aerobics program, it's time to look into the specific exercises. If you've ever done any yoga or calisthenics, many of these exercises—or variations of them—will be familiar to you. You will find, however, that doing these movements in the water is a little different from doing them in a gym or on a mat in your home. The resistance of the water, as I've already explained, will add an extra fitness dimension to the movements, and generally speaking, you'll find that your muscles are more cooperative in the water than they are on land. If you're like me, you'll simply *enjoy* the exercises more. They won't seem like work.

The exercises described throughout this chapter are self-explanatory, but let me make a few observations about the exercises in general before I get into the specifics.

First of all, do not let the simplicity of some of the exercises deceive you into thinking that they are not as beneficial as some of the more complicated calisthenics you may have done in other exercise programs. Keep in mind the added effectiveness the resistance of the water gives to each of these exercises.

Second, it's important that unless it's otherwise indicated, you do the movements in these exercises quickly. The faster you do most of these exercises, the greater the resistance value of the water.

Finally, if you begin to feel any pain in any of the exercises, don't force it. I don't subscribe to the "no pain, no gain" notion that you sometimes hear from people who run other exercise programs. None of these exercises should hurt, although you should experience the burning sensation that comes from the build-up of lactic acid I talked about in the last chapter. If you feel pain, it's your body telling you that you shouldn't be doing that particular exercise and that it might be time to consult a doctor.

Breathing

Unless I've indicated otherwise, you should try to breathe as normally as possible during these exercises. Let the demand of the exercise dictate how much oxygen you need to take in. Resist the temptation—more common than you may think—to hold your breath, and pay particularly close attention to the exhale, making sure you've gotten rid of all the waste products that build when you're exercising vigorously.

THE WARM-UP

Although water in and of itself can serve to loosen the muscles, I still recommend very strongly that you precede each workout with a brief warm-up period. The warm-up that follows consists of some basic stretches that will loosen all the muscles in your body. These stretches are similar to those recommended for runners and other athletes, and the important thing is to do each of *these* exercises slowly, as opposed to most of the others in the program. Except for the floor stretches in the following group, you can do these in or out of the water.

THE WAIST BEND

Benefit: *Loosens the lower back and hamstrings.*

1. Stand with your feet a comfortable distance apart, your hands relaxed at your side.

2. Bend slowly at the waist, your hands dropping naturally, until you feel some strain in the back of your legs. Don't try to touch your toes; simply let your body hang as far as it can.

3. Maintaining your position, cradle your arms and drop your head, allowing the weight of your head to extend hamstring muscles naturally.

THE TRUNK TWIST

Benefit: *Loosens the muscles in the lower back and abdomen.*

1. **Stand with your feet about a foot apart with your hands on your hips.**

2. **Keeping your feet planted and your head facing forward, rotate your trunk clockwise until your left elbow is pointing forward. Hold for a few seconds.**

3. **Rotate counter-clockwise so that your right elbow is pointing forward.**

THE ANKLE STRETCH

Benefit: *Stretches ankles and calves (very important for swimmers because of the flexibility needed for kicking).*

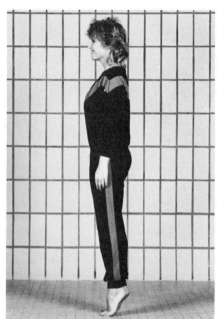

2. Raise your feet until you're standing on tiptoes and hold for several seconds.

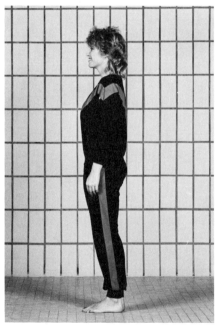

1. Stand erect with your feet together and your hands at your sides.

3. Return to starting position.

THE REACH AND GRAB

Benefit: *Stretches shoulder and upper arm muscles.*

1. **Stand with your feet to-gether, one arm at your side and the other raised straight above you.**

2. **Make a fist and extend the raised arm as high as you can, keeping your feet firmly on the ground. Repeat with other arm.**

Keep your body as straight as possible in this stretch but not rigid.

THE SHOULDER ROLL

Benefit: Loosens the muscles in the shoulders and upper back and eliminates tension from the neck.

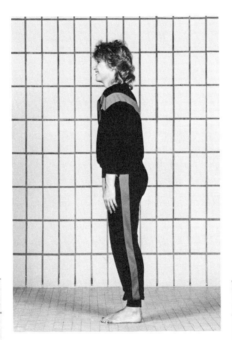

2. **Keeping your hands at your sides, bring both shoulders forward until you build up tension in the muscles just beneath the shoulders.**

1. **Stand comfortably with your feet about a shoulder's width apart.**

3. **Slowly and evenly roll your shoulders up and back until you've completed a circle. Keep your arms and hands still: Let the shoulders do the work.**

THE NECK TURN

Benefit: Releases tension and loosens neck muscles.

1. Stand with your hands on your hips, your feet about a foot apart.

2. Keeping your shoulders facing front, turn your head slowly to the left as far as you can until you're looking over your shoulder.

3. Return to starting position. Repeat the same movement in the opposite direction.

THE DOUBLE-WING STRETCH

Benefit: Stretches the chest muscles (pectorals), the back, the upper arms, and the shoulders.

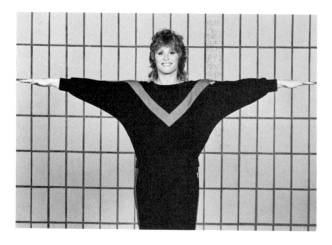

1. Stand with your hands extended straight out to the sides.

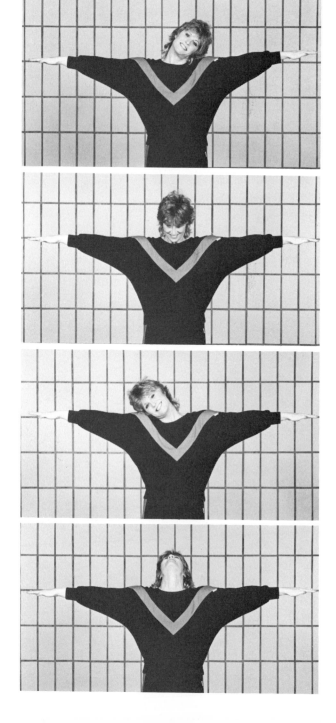

2. Create a slow, wide circle with your head, keeping your body straight, your arms extended, and your neck as loose as possible.

THE BACK SCRATCH

Benefit: *Stretches shoulder muscles and upper back.*

2. Take your right hand and bring it directly behind you, past your right ear and try to touch the outstretched fingers of your left hand. If you can't actually touch, try to get as close as possible.

1. Stand comfortably with your hands locked behind your back.

3. Repeat with reversed arm position.

THE LEG TUCK

Benefit: Stretches out the lower spine.

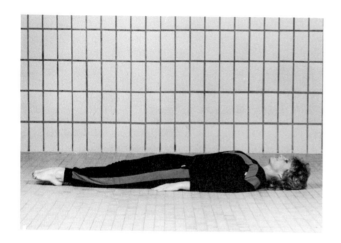

1. Lie on your back on the pool deck.

2. Keeping your head and shoulders on the ground, roll back slightly and grasp both knees with your hands.

3. Pull your knees back to your chest and hold that position for about ten seconds.

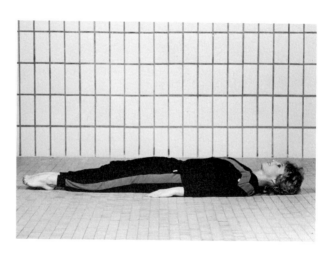

4. Slowly return to starting position.

(Note: This is an optional stretch for people who have had a history of back problems.)

THE LEG TUCK AND RAISE

Benefit: *Stretches spine and lower back.*

1. Lie on your back with your arms at your sides and your palms flat against the ground.

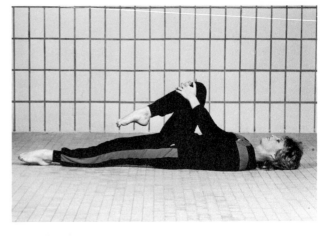

2. Bend your right knee and grasp it with both hands.

3. Try to straighten your leg as high as you can, keeping your foot flexed and your other leg flat against the ground.

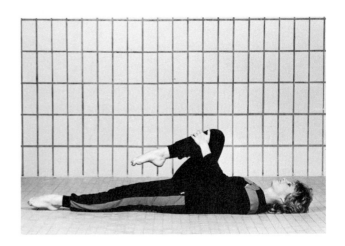

4. Bend the knee toward your chest and return to starting position. Repeat with other leg.

THE COBRA STRETCH

Benefit: *Stretches abdomen and lower back.*

1. Sit in a kneeling position: your back straight, your buttocks resting on your heels, and your hands on your knees.

2. Curl your body forward, keeping your buttocks against your heels. Your hands and elbows should be flat against the ground (your elbows next to your knees), and your head should just about touch the ground.

3. Using your hands to support you, slide your legs straight behind you, creating a bow in the middle of your back.

4. Bring your legs back under you again and return to the "curl" position.

BOBBING

Bobbing is one of the simplest of all the Hydro-Aerobics exercises in the program, but it may well be the most important. For not only does bobbing help strengthen and tone the body in general, it enables you to practice—and master—the proper breathing habits so fundamental to good swimming. (And more swimmers than you can imagine—even competitive swimmers—are their own worst enemies in the water because they don't know how—or actually forget—to breathe properly.)

The Basic Bobbing Movement

You can bob in water as shallow as four feet or as deep as ten feet, but the ideal depth is one at which your head is just beneath the water surface. There are different types of bobs, and I know swimmers who've made up their own variations, but the key to all bobbing is nothing more complicated than a simple knee bend. You bend your knees on the way down. You straighten them on the way up.

Breathing and Bobbing

The basic idea behind the breathing aspect of bobbing is to keep it controlled and rhythmic, the same way you would breathe if you were actually swimming. You don't *need* to submerge your head in the water with each bob, but I recommend submersion because doing so enables you to simulate more closely the breathing pattern you would follow if you were actually swimming.

The tricky part of breathing when you bob is making sure your head emerges from the water at *precisely* the moment you are out of air. And you shouldn't be out of breath at this point—simply out of air. The idea behind bobbing is not to see how long you can keep your head under without breathing. The idea is to set up an easy breathing pattern in which your breathing is naturally coordinated with your movement. This coordination, of course, is what you strive for when you're actually swimming, but if you can't achieve it when you're working on a simple bob, you're not going to be able to do it when you're doing one of the more complicated stroking movements.

Bobbing Step by Step

1. Begin by taking in a breath that is perhaps twice as deep as the breath you would normally take but doesn't use all your lung capacity. (Some instructors suggest that you take in a pint of air, but how do you measure a pint of air? It beats me.)

2. Drop straight down into the water by bending your knees and start to exhale as soon as your face enters the water, forcing the air from both your nose and your mouth. If you want to, you can extend your arms and try to bring your knees to your chest under water.

3. Resurface by straightening your knees, exhaling as soon as your head emerges from the water.

How to Practice Bobbing

Here are a few tips to help you bob more effectively.

1. **Concentration.** Before you even begin to bob, spend a minute or two concentrating on your breathing. Remember, you want to breathe somewhat more deeply than normal, but you don't want to do *deep* breathing in the normal sense of the term.

2. **The exhale.** Once you've established what you think is the proper breathing rhythm (and you might have to make some adjustments), work next on the exhale. You don't have to bob just yet. Simply submerge your head in the water and get used to exhaling *all* the breath, not explosively but steadily and easily. Start with a three count (1, 2, 3 and out of the water, breathe 2, 3, and back in the water). Do this until you can repeat it several times without feeling yourself losing breath.

3. **The bob itself.** Once you've focused on your breathing, you're ready to incorporate this breathing rhythm with the bobbing movement. As I said earlier, the depth of the water isn't crucial. It's just a little more complicated to bob when the water isn't over your head. If you're bobbing in shallow water, you simply bend your knees until your head is just beneath the surface. If the water is deeper, you let your body slip, knifelike, into the water until you either touch bottom or, if the water is a little deeper, as soon as your head is completely submerged. To emerge from the water, depending on the depth, you either straighten your legs and push off from the bottom or else push downward with your hands.

Problems to Expect

If you are bobbing correctly, you should never—that's right, *never*—run out of breath. Why? Because you are breathing as you would if you were reading a book or driving a car.

If you find yourself struggling for breath, it means one of three things: one, you're not emptying your lungs sufficiently when you're in the water (which means that when you come to the surface you have to exhale quickly and then gulp for air); two, you're keeping your head under the water a second or two too long; or three, you haven't attained the proper breathing rhythm.

You may also find when you start to practice bobbing that after a few bobs, you get a little dizzy. Don't worry. It only means that your breaths are a little too deep and your brain is getting more oxygen than it needs. Keep in mind that you don't *need* a great deal of oxygen to do this exercise. Take in less air, and the problem should disappear.

THE EXERCISES

Each of the exercises in the Hydro-Aerobics Programs is designed to promote both flexibility and muscle tone. If you want to concentrate on building more strength, use special "floaties" to increase the water resistance.

Legs, Hips, Thighs, and Buttocks

Each of the exercises in this series will tone, stretch, and strengthen the muscles in your lower and upper legs and, in some cases, your buttocks.

THE LEG CROSSOVER

Benefit: *Firms your inner and outer thigh muscles and trims your hips.*

1. **Position yourself with your back against the pool wall and your hands extended to the sides, grasping the edge.**

2. **Extend your legs straight out in front and then swing them apart. (Use your stomach muscles to supply the thrust of this movement.)**

3. Cross your left leg over right leg and then swing it back.

4. Repeat the same movement, this time crossing your right leg over your left leg.

The first time you try this exercise you may run into a couple of difficulties. If you have a lean build, for instance, you could have trouble keeping your legs from sinking. Should this happen, try arching your back and tilting your neck back a little. You might also find it a little difficult, if you've never worked on your arm muscles, to hold on to the wall. With a little practice, you should be able to do this exercise easily. You might also find the ladder helpful, enabling you to gain a better grip.

FRONT AND BACK LEG RAISE

Benefit: *Tones and strengthens the muscles in the lower portion of the thigh and the lower back.*

1. Stand in water waist to chest high, with your side to the pool wall. With your left hand holding the wall for support, raise your right leg and extend it in front of you. Keep your foot pointed.

2. Swing the leg down and back until you've taken it as far back as you can in an arabesque position. Repeat with the other leg.

The slower and more controlled you are throughout this exercise, the better, particularly when you're pulling your leg back through the water.

THE SIDE LEG RAISE

Benefit: Tones and strengthens the inner thighs.

2. **Lift leg out to the side, keeping your knee straight.**

1. **Stand an arm's distance away from the wall and take hold of the edge with both hands.**

3. **Press the leg down through the water, feeling the tension in your inner thighs. Repeat with the other leg.**

DONKEY KICK

Benefit: Tones the upper thighs and buttocks.

2. Keeping your leg firmly
   planted, swing your other
   leg straight up as if you
   were mounting a horse.

1. Stand an arm's distance
   away from the pool wall
   on one leg and grasp the
   edge of the wall with both
   hands.

3. Return to starting position
   and repeat with other leg.

THIGH PULL

Benefit: Stretches and tones the quadriceps (the large muscles in
the front of the thigh).

2. Lift your left leg behind
   you, grasp it around the
   ankles with your left arm.

1. Stand in water about waist
   deep (you can hold on to
   the side of the pool if you
   like).

3. Maintaining an erect position, pull your leg inward
   so that your knee is pointing to the bottom of the
   pool. Repeat with other
   leg.

THE SIDE KNEE BEND

Benefit: *Strengthens and tones the entire leg.*

1. Stand in a "lunge" position, with one leg bent and the other extended straight to the side. Your weight should be on the bent leg.

2. Keeping your body straight, shift your weight to the opposite leg, bending that leg and straightening the other.

3. Return to starting position and repeat.

(This exercise is the Hydro-Aerobics version of the familiar knee bend, and what's interesting about it is that people who wouldn't be able to do regular knee bends because of problem knees can usually do the Hydro-Aerobics version very safely.)

THE WALKING TOE TOUCH

*Benefit: Strengthens and firms the calves and the thighs,
with very little risk of strain.*

**2. Step forward with your
right leg, raising it at least
waist high with your knee
straight. As you walk,
reach out to touch the outstretched foot with the
same hand.**

**1. Stand in water about waist
level, with your arms
straight in front of you.**

**3. Repeat the movement with
the other leg.**

(Do this exercise rapidly but try to keep
your movements as smooth as possible.)

Abdominals

Swimming in and of itself does a good job of stretching the abdominal muscles, but if you have a problem with bulges in your midsection, you'll have to do two things: one, cut back your caloric intake (your midsection and rear section are your body's favorite depositories for fat); and two, work on exercises specifically aimed at toning the midsection.

THE WALKING WAIST TWIST

Benefit: *Similar to the walking toe touch, but with an added wrinkle that will tighten your waist and midsection.*

1. With your hands locked behind your head, raise your right leg (knee bent) and try to touch your knee and your *left* elbow.

2. Repeat the same movement with the other leg and elbow.

To get the best results with this exercise, keep your toes pointed downward as you raise your knees.

THE POOLSIDE SIT-UP

Benefit: Similar to the land version of the sit-up in that it tightens abdominal muscles as much as the land version does.

1. Stand in any depth water with your back to the side of the pool and take hold of the gutter with both hands.

2. When you've found a comfortable position for your arms (and it's not all that easy), tuck your knees together, bring them up to your chest, and hold that position for a slow count of five. Return to starting position and repeat.

THE SIT-UP AND THRUST

Benefit: *A variation of the sit-up that puts added pressure on your lower back. (If you've had a history of back trouble, be careful.)*

2. **Lower your knees until your thighs are roughly parallel to the water surface.**

1. **Raise your knees as you did for the poolside sit-up.**

3. **Straighten your knees until your body is lying flat in the water.**

As a variation on this exercise, you can kick your legs, scissors style, when they're extended.

THE PIKE AND STRETCH

Benefit: This is a somewhat advanced exercise, but it's terrific for tightening your abdominals.

1. Position yourself against the wall of the pool, with the top hand grasping the edge, the palm of the lower hand flat against the wall, and your legs extended.

2. Lower your legs slowly, making sure you keep them straight and together. You should feel the tension in your stomach.

3. Extend your legs slowly behind you so that you're in a prone position.

THE SIDEWINDER

Benefit: *Tightens abdomen and upper thighs.*

1. Assume a prone floating position, with one hand on top of the pool edge and the palm of the other hand a foot below it.

2. Swing both legs around until you touch the pool wall. Repeat the same movement on other side.

THE SIDE BEND

Benefit: *This is one of my favorite exercises, because it not only tones the midriff but also has fun movements.*

2. Holding on to the side of the pool, lean as far as you can toward the middle. Tilt your neck and arm back toward the pool wall.

1. Stand sideways to the pool wall, with your feet about a foot away from the wall and the far hand extended upward.

3. Swing your lower body back toward the pool wall until your hips touch and extend your arms and neck the other way.

Arms, Shoulders, and Chest

This series of exercises is designed to strengthen and tone the muscles in your shoulders, arms, and to a lesser extent, your chest. Each exercise can be done with your hands alone or, even better, with hand paddles to increase the resistance. In either case, make sure you do the movements rapidly and vigorously.

THE HAND PRESS

Benefit: Strengthens upper arms and pectorals.

1. **Stand in water about chest high with your hands, forming an X (palms outward), submerged a few inches in the water in front of you.**

2. **Pull your arms as vigorously as you can to your right, bending slightly but otherwise holding your position solid. Make sure fingers are slightly spread and that you keep your hands just beneath the surface.**

3. **Repeat the same movement to the other side.**

The key to getting the most out of this exercise is maintaining the X-pattern with your hands, generating as much resistance as possible with your open palm.

THE ARM PRESS

Benefit: Strengthens shoulders, upper arms, and pectorals.

1. Hold a soccer or water polo ball directly in front of you so that it's floating lightly on the surface.

2. Pull it down to your left side as vigorously as you can and hold for a few seconds before pulling it back toward the surface. Repeat the same movement on the other side.

THE LADDER PULL

Benefit: *The pool ladder can be an excellent aid for strengthening your arms. Use it as long as it doesn't inconvenience the other swimmers.*

2. Push off the wall with your feet so that your legs and arms are extended.

1. Take hold of the ladder with both hands and sit back in the water, your knees slightly bent.

3. Using your arms only, pull yourself back to the original position.

ONE ARM LADDER PULL

Benefit: Strengthens shoulders and midriff.

2. Take your left arm and reach back across your head, as if you were trying to grab hold of the ladder.

1. With your feet together and against the pool wall, take hold of the ladder with your right hand and let yourself stretch out into the water.

3. Swivel your hips toward the pool wall and extend your arm toward the other side of the pool.

THE BREASTSTROKE PULL

Benefit: *Simulates the arm pull of the breaststroke, a stroke that helps build strength and tone in your upper arms and shoulders.*

1. **Stand in water that's about waist deep with your hands straight in front of you, resting on the surface of the water.**

2. **Pull your hands down through the water (palms facing one another) until you've extended your arms fully behind you.**

THE ARM CROSS

Benefit: Strengthens and tones upper arms and shoulders.

2. **Press each arm straight down so that they cross in front of you, keeping both close to the body.**

1. **Using floaties (optional) stand in water about chest high, bend slightly at the waist, and extend your arms to the side with hands just beneath the surface of the water.**

3. **Return your arms (keeping your palms facing each other) to the starting position.**

THE POOLSIDE PUSH-UP

Benefit: Strengthens triceps, biceps, and shoulder muscles.

1. Stand in the water facing the side of the pool with your palms flat against the top ledge and your knees bent.

2. With your knees slightly bent, jump up until your arms are extended, supporting the weight of your body. See if you can hold that position for a long count of three.

3. Return to starting position very slowly and repeat.

The Cool-Down

The purpose of these two cool-down exercises is to loosen whatever tightness has been built up through the course of the routine. They are stretches that you can do either in or out of the water, and they can go a long way to reduce the feeling of stiffness you sometimes have after a vigorous workout.

THE TOTAL BODY STRETCH

1. **Crouch in water about chest deep and raise your arms.**

2. **Keeping your feet firmly on the ground, straighten your knees, lift your arms straight up in the air, and arch your back very slowly.**

THE PUSH-OFF

1. Holding on to the gutter with both hands, tuck your knees up underneath and place your feet against the side of the wall, just beneath the water level.

2. Holding firmly to the gutter, try to straighten your legs as much as possible. When you reach the end of the stretch, hold for at least twenty seconds.

A Muscle Glossary

Here are some of the technical terms used to describe various muscles in the body.

Biceps—Muscle located in the front portion of the upper arm.

Deltoid—Triangular muscle that covers the shoulder joint.

Gluteus—Buttocks muscle.

Gluteus maximus—Largest of the buttocks muscles.

Gluteus minimus—You guessed it: smallest of the buttocks muscles.

Gracilis—Located in the inner part of thigh; the muscle that controls the movement of the legs toward one another.

Intercostals—Muscles located between the ribs.

Pectorals—Chest or breast muscles.

Quadriceps—Large muscle in the front portion of the thigh.

Trapezius—Muscle that lies between your neck and shoulder bone.

Triceps—Muscle in the back portion of the upper arm.

4· BECOMING A BETTER SWIMMER

Y ou do not have to be an accomplished swimmer to derive
the full benefit, mentally and physically, from Hydro-Aerobics. That's one of the nicest features of the program. On the
other hand, much of the enjoyment and satisfaction Hydro-
Aerobics has to offer come from the sense of personal achieve-
ment you can realize as you see yourself improving as a swimmer
with each workout. And by improving, I don't necessarily mean
swimming faster but swimming more smoothly, more gracefully,
and with more confidence.

If you're happy with the way you're swimming right now,
you can skip this chapter and go on to the workouts themselves,
but I would urge you to at least skim this chapter. As strong a
swimmer as you might be, you may just pick up one or two tips
that could make a big difference in some of your strokes.

The Basics of Good Swimming

There are certain basic scientific principles that apply to all the
strokes in swimming. Maybe you've heard of them, maybe not.
But before we look at the individual strokes, let's look at some
of these basic principles. I'll try not to spoil your fun by getting
too technical.

Buoyancy

Buoyancy refers to the tendency of some objects—the human
body, for instance—to float instead of sink when submerged in
the water. The principle behind buoyancy is that water, like any

71

liquid, exerts pressure equally at all times around a submerged object and that the pressure increases the deeper you submerge the object.

This means that at any given time the top layer of any object in the water is exerting less pressure downward than is being exerted upward (the reason being that the bottom layer is deeper in the water and thus has more pressure operating against it). And it is this difference in pressure—more pressure upward than downward—that makes objects buoyant and tends to keep them afloat.

There's another factor at work in buoyancy, and it has to do with the density of an object—how heavy it is in relationship to its size and volume—and the density of the water. And this factor explains why certain objects—a beach ball, for instance—are more buoyant than other objects—a brick, for instance.

But let's not complicate matters too much. The important point to bear in mind about buoyancy is that most people are naturally buoyant (although the leaner and more muscular you are, the less buoyant you tend to be), so that once your body is partially submerged, the natural force of buoyancy is likely to keep you afloat. And this natural tendency to float means that you don't have to struggle to stay afloat but that you are actually *in* the water and not on top of it. The distinction is important, because the position of your body in the water is one of the keys to efficient swimming. When you try to fight the natural laws of buoyancy, you end up actually fighting yourself in the water.

The Resistance Principle

The so-called resistance principle in swimming is based on Newton's third law of motion, which, if you remember from your high school science, is that for every action there is an equal and opposite reaction. If you apply this law to swimming, you can understand why, if you want to propel yourself forward in the water, you have to pull your hands and arms backward through the water, or toward you.

But there's a problem here. For as you begin to press the water backward, you start the water moving in a backward direction as well, which serves to *reduce* the pressure you're encountering as you push. And as the resistance you meet lessens, you cut down on the forward thrust you can generate by the pressure.

The question, then, is how you continue to find the resistance necessary to propel yourself forward when the very movement designed to take advantage of this resistance tends to reduce it. And the answer is that your hands should never pull straight back in the water but, rather, should move in a slightly elliptical pattern. This way your hands avoid water that's moving backward and instead come up against water that is stationary. The result: resistance stays constant, and you are able to maintain your forward thrust.

The Importance of Staying Streamlined

Swimming is no different from dancing, running, or just about any sport you can think of from baseball to tennis to gymnastics. You do it best when you're relaxed and when your body is coordinated. But there is a basic principle that applies to swimming and swimming alone, and it's one I'm going to keep coming back to time and again as we go through each of the basic strokes. It's known as *streamlining*.

Streamlining refers to the position of your body as you're swimming, and the idea behind the principle is to keep your body positioned in the water so that you limit the amount of frontal resistance.

The way you limit this frontal resistance is to keep your body as prone (that is, as parallel to the surface of the water) as possible. The more prone—streamlined—you can keep your body in the water, the less resistance your body is going to create as you move forward in the water. But the minute your legs begin to drop, the resistance increases. (That's why you can swim so much faster in the water than you can run in it.)

There are several keys to keeping your body streamlined, but the most important consideration by far is making sure your head is *in* the water as you are swimming and that when you breathe you do so by *turning* your head and not by lifting it out of the water.

Right

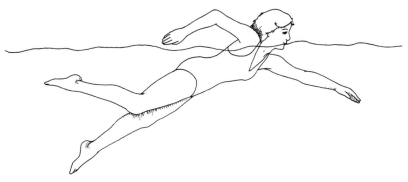

Wrong

The logic is this: When your head is out of the water, especially when you're craning your neck to keep it out of the water, the natural gravity of your body will pull your legs down and cause you to sink; that's basic physics. Put your head into the water, on the other hand, and not only do your legs and hips come up, but your body now becomes more streamlined and much easier to pull through the water.

The analogy I like to use when I talk about streamlining is that of a speedboat. Think of your legs, ankles, and feet as the motor and your head as the bow. If you keep this image in mind, you can see why it's important for your face to be in the water, with the surface of the water breaking at the tip of your forehead. In this position a strong kick will force you through the water, the way a motor powers a speedboat, and your head will break the water in front of you to make an air pocket. Then you can turn your head ever so slightly to the side to take advantage of the air pocket and take a breath.

Kicking

Some swimming instructors downplay the importance of kicking and will tell you that the function of the kick in swimming—particularly in the crawl—isn't so much to propel you through the water as it is to stabilize your body position. The theory has long been that whatever energy you might expend on the kick to give you propulsion is more efficiently spent on your arms.

I see the logic behind the theory, but I don't subscribe to it. I've always concentrated on my kick, particularly when I was swimming competitively, and I think that as a recreational swimmer, especially someone who is swimming to improve flexibility and muscle tone, your legs should do their share of the work.

I'll talk about the specifics of the various kicking motions in swimming when we run down the individual strokes, but let me stress here the basic principle behind kicking: The idea is to stay fluid and rhythmic with each kick and not to see how much water you can splash on the side of the pool. In other words, it's not power that you're looking for when you kick, it's smoothness. A second principle is that an efficient swimming kick involves the *entire* leg and not just the lower part, which is the way many swimmers do it. You should kick from your hips, not from your knees.

Breathing

If there is any one aspect of swimming that creates the most difficulty for most people, it's breathing—and for obvious reasons. You can't take breathing for granted when you swim, the way you do for nonwater sports. You have to breathe *efficiently*, and you have to coordinate your breathing with other movements in your strokes.

Here, again, even though I'll be talking about some of the specifics that relate to breathing when I look into the individual strokes, let me stress three of the basic principles that apply to *all* strokes.

The first principle—one I've already mentioned briefly when I talked about streamlining—is that you must learn to keep your head *in* the water as you breathe out, relying on a slight turn (and not a lift) of the head when the time comes to inhale. If you keep lifting your head from the water in order to breathe in, or if you try to keep your head out of the water throughout the entire stroke, you'll compromise your body position and you'll have to work that much harder—and less efficiently—to generate movement.

The second principle is that you have to rely almost entirely on your mouth when you breathe, and the only reason I say "almost" is that you'll rely on your nose somewhat when you're exhaling. *Never*, however, do you use your nose for inhaling when you swim.

Finally, you must learn to time your breaths in relation to other components of the stroke. How often you take breaths—and when—will depend not only on the distance you're swimming (when you're swimming longer distances, you breathe more frequently), but also on the stroke, on your condition, and, in the end, on what works best for you. The important consideration, as we'll see, is rhythm and consistency.

An Experiment in Breathing

If there is any one key to breathing in swimming, it's letting out all the air *underneath* the water. If you don't, when you turn your head to the side and breathe, you have to let out the remaining air before you take in new air, and you'll also force a hesitation in the cycle of your pull and create a hitch in your stroke.

If you suspect that you don't breathe efficiently when you swim, here's a little experiment that could prove helpful to you.

1. Stand in the shallow end of the pool, hold your nose, and submerge your head. Keeping your head submerged, let go of your nose at brief intervals simply to get used to the feeling.

2. The second part of the experiment is to take a deep breath through your mouth on the surface, then submerge your head as you blow out of your nose and then your mouth. Make sure you push all the air out of your lungs before you come up for the next mouthful of air.

Once you've mastered the breathing technique when you're *not* swimming, it's much easier to incorporate it into your stroke.

5· THE BASIC STROKES

The crawl stroke—usually referred to as freestyle but also called the Australian crawl—is the bread-and-butter stroke of swimming, the stroke most instructors like to teach before any other. One reason for this is that it is the fastest of the strokes (although some think that within a few years world-class butterfly swimmers will be able to outrace freestylers). A second reason is that once you've mastered the basic coordination of the crawl, the other strokes become that much easier. Finally, the crawl is probably the smoothest and most rhythmic of all the strokes, and if you can do it well, probably the most enjoyable to do.

All the basics we talked about in the last section apply to the crawl, but let's look at the stroke in a little more detail.

Your ultimate goal when you're swimming freestyle is to be as fluid as possible. You enhance the fluidity of your stroke by keeping your body streamlined and flat, by kicking and breathing properly, and finally, by properly timing the kick and the arm pull.

Are you a little overwhelmed? Don't be. I'm going to break down these elements one by one and then give you a routine that should help you develop the fluidity that is your goal.

Body Position

Two aspects of your stroke above all will determine how flat and streamlined you remain as you do each crawl stroke. The first is the position of your head. The second is your kick. If your head is too high (something that will always happen if you don't keep your head in the water when you breathe out), your body from the hips down is going to drop down into the water, increasing the drag and forcing you to work that much harder with your arms. If your kick lacks efficiency, your body will shimmy too much in the water, producing a different but no less troublesome form of drag. Streamlining, in other words, isn't something you can consciously achieve on its own. Instead, it results from your head position and your kick.

The Kick

The mistake most people make when they swim the crawl is to rely almost solely on the *lower* leg for the kicking motion. That's why inexperienced swimmers will splash so much more water than experienced swimmers. Experienced swimmers know that the crawl should be done with the entire leg, from the hip down to the toes.

Here are the checkpoints to remember:

Knees. Your knees should be relaxed but shouldn't really bend much. The hips and thighs should be doing the bulk of the work, and for a good reason: That's where you find your largest and strongest muscles.

Feet. Your feet should be slightly arched, with toes pointing outward. The reason I say "slightly" is that while you need a slight arch to stabilize your body position, you need to keep your ankles loose and flexible. Otherwise you put extra pressure on your leg muscles.

Leg position. Keep your legs as close together as possible without actually touching. The farther apart your legs are, the harder you'll have to work to generate forward movement.

Size of the kick. Different swimming instructors have differing views on how big a kick you should make. Some will tell you to make the kick as large as two feet. Others recommend a kick about half that size. My view is that you don't need all that big a kick to be effective, so I think you should make your kick about the same size as your normal stride when you're walking. For most people, this will be between 12 and 18 inches (longer, of course, if you have longer legs). The point is not to confuse the size of the kick with the efficiency of the kick. You'd be amazed at how much you can get out of even a 10-inch kick if you're doing it properly.

Speed of the kick. The speed of your kick is important, since the faster you kick, the more speed you're going to generate, but more important than the speed is the manner in which you coordinate the kick with the arm pull.

The Arm Pull

Since most of your propulsion in the water comes from the arm pull or stroke, it's logical that your speed will be directly affected by the efficiency of your arm movements. Most amateur swimmers, in my experience, do not employ an efficient arm pull, and usually for one of two reasons:

First, improper hand position; many people cup their wrists too severely or twist their hands at strange angles. Improper stroking pattern; many (correct that; most) people have too straight down an arm pull rather than the diagonal pattern we'll talk about in a minute.

In a word, "resistance." You need to *feel* the resistance of the water as you pull. If you don't, you are either the strongest person in the world or you're not doing the pull properly. No matter what condition I was in during competition, I was always aware of the water resisting me as I pulled through it and could feel the water resisting me as I pressed through, and I was able to use that feel to correct my mechanics and increase my speed.

A

B

C

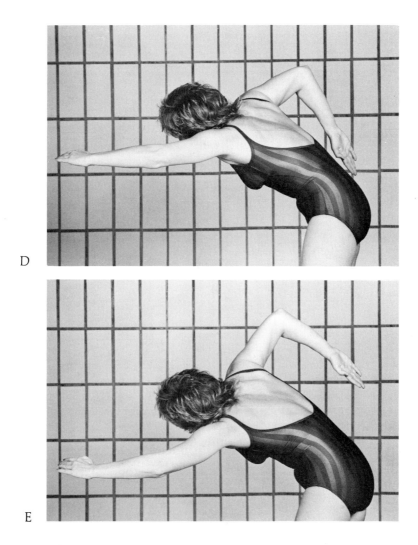

D

E

This sequence illustrates an efficient arm pull for the crawl. Notice the angle of the elbow in photos B and C. That's the "lever"
effect you should try to achieve. Notice also that my right shoulder (D) rolls back slightly and my right hand is above even with
my hips.

The Hand Position

Let's start with fingers. Your little finger should always enter the water first and your thumb last. This means that your fingers should never be pointing straight in front of you as you swim. Instead each of your hands should be angled slightly outward. Despite what you may have been told when you were younger, you don't have to hold your fingers too tightly together when you're pulling. The air pockets between the fingers will actually aid in cupping the water. Besides, if you concentrate too much on keeping your fingers together you usually end up making your arms too stiff.

As for *where* your hands should enter the water, the most efficient point is roughly on a line parallel with your shoulders. The distance between the point at which your right hand enters the water and your left hand enters the water, in other words, should always be approximately the width of your shoulders.

The Press

The press portion of the pull should begin as soon as your hand enters the water, and the most important thing is to make sure your elbow is bent as you pull. Think of your arm as a lever, with your elbow following the wrist. It's almost as if you're doing a push-up in the water, except that your ultimate strength comes from your back muscles. It helps, too, if you concentrate on *rolling* your shoulder into the water as the elbow enters. As Olympics coach George Hanes once said, you should imagine that you're reaching over a barrel and pulling it underneath your body.

At the end of the pull, you should be pushing as hard as you can at your thighs. The recovery portion of the stroke should be relaxed, with the elbow coming out of the water first and then following the hand as it enters the water for the next pull.

If you make it a point to keep your eyes and head directly forward (except, of course, when you're breathing), you'll find it much easier to keep your body streamlined. But keeping your head level is not as easy as it seems. There is a natural tendency to tilt your head to the left or right side, which will lead you to favor one of your arms and make it that much more difficult to maintain a smooth, fluid stroke.

Timing the Kick and Pull

A lot of swimmers worry unnecessarily about counting the number of kicks per pull cycle (the time it takes for both arms to complete the stroke), but the fact of the matter is that no single pattern works for every swimmer. The Australian Shane Gould, a gold medalist in the 200-meter and 400-meter freestyle in the 1972 Olympics, was a two-beat kicker, while Keena Rothhammer, a gold medalist in the 1980 100-meter freestyle, was a six-beat kicker. The most important consideration in the timing is to make sure the kick stabilizes your stroke and keeps your body on *top* of the water, so you can execute the arm pull effectively.

The Backstroke

The backstroke is the one stroke in which you can work on your tan (assuming you swim outdoors, of course) and get a workout at the same time. But it's difficult to do smoothly and gracefully, and it's one stroke in which you need to be especially flexible in your upper arms and shoulders. Let's look at the basics.

Body Position

Both your back and your neck should be reasonably straight throughout the backstroke, but not so rigid that you fight your own progress. The top of your hips should not be much more than a hand's length beneath the surface. Get them any deeper and you'll increase the drag. You'll assure the proper hip position if you keep your head reasonably straight (imagine yourself lying flat on a raft). If you crane your head too far back, your hips are going to rise. Tuck your chin in too much, and your hips will go deeper.

The Arm Pull

The arm pull is, for most people, the hardest thing about the backstroke. First of all, to get the most out of it, you need plenty of range of motion in your shoulders (the shoulder stretch warm-up exercise is especially important for this stroke). Second, the movement itself is fairly complex and gives even some experienced swimmers the fits.

Many swimmers mistakenly use a windmill type motion on the arm pull, but the proper stroke is more akin to a throw—make that *two* throws. By that I mean your elbow begins in an extended position on the backstroke pull, bends to about ninety degrees midway through the pull, and then extends again as your arm is coming upward.

The best way to get a feel for the right-arm pull on the backstroke is to go through the motion outside the pool. Here's the procedure I recommend:

1. Stand with right arm extended straight above you (imagine as you're doing this that you're lying faceup in the water) and the other at your side.

2. Pull your right shoulder backward in a slightly circular motion, keeping your arm straight and lifting your left arm up at the same time.

3. Once your right hand begins to drop below your shoulder, your elbow will bend naturally. Let it do so and then straighten it gradually so that by the time your arm passes the hip, your arm will be fully extended.

If you're having trouble executing this arm pull, visualize a clock. At the twelve o'clock section, your arms are fully extended. At three o'clock, your elbows are at their sharpest bend, and at six o'clock they're extended again.

As far as the mechanics of the motion go, here are the key points:

1. Bend your elbow *as soon as* you pull your arm down and back.
2. Increase the bend until you're halfway through the pull.
3. Keep the elbow straight throughout the rest of the pull.

Once you've mastered the basic movement, you're ready to execute the entire pull. Your arms should be moving continuously (there is no glide) and at cross purposes: As one hand enters the water above your head, the other hand should be coming out of the water at your hip. Make sure you keep your elbows as close to your body as you can manage as you pull through, and even though your elbows are straight, try to keep your arms—especially the wrists—relaxed.

Hand Position

Hand position is extremely important throughout the backstroke. Your hand should enter the water in a knifelike position, wrist slightly back, but as soon as you submerge the hand, you need to position the palm flat against the water as you pull upward. Keep the thumb up and your fingers close together but not glued together.

The Kick

You use essentially the same kick for the backstroke—the flutter kick—that you do for the crawl. The only difference, apart from the difference in body position, is that you kick a little more rapidly. The same basic principles are important: keeping your legs slightly bent, using the entire leg and not just the lower leg, and above all, staying rhythmic. Your ankles should be extended, just as they are in the crawl, and shouldn't dip more than two feet beneath the surface; and the distance between the feet on the kick should never be more than 12 to 18 inches. Another thing: your feet should never come out of the water. If your kick gets too high, remember, your body will tilt backward.

Probably the biggest mistake you can make during the backstroke kick is to bend your knees too much during the down part of the kick, which means the upper leg doesn't get involved enough in the kick. It's not an easy thing to control, but if you concentrate on using your thigh on the down kick, you'll avoid the problem.

How often you choose to kick with each stroke is up to you. Some backstrokers will kick as few as two beats per cycle; others will kick as many as six.

Breathing

Because your head is never submerged in the backstroke, you might think that breathing is unimportant. Breathing, in fact, can cause you more problems on the backstroke than it can with any other stroke, for there is a tendency to breathe too quickly, so that your oxygen intake suffers and you tire more easily.

My advice is to establish from the beginning an easy rhythmic breathing pattern, inhaling as one arm is coming out of the water and exhaling as the other arm is coming out of the water.

Putting It All Together

I recommend the same general system of coordinating arms and legs on the backstroke as when you're swimming freestyle. As in the freestyle, I like to see swimmers use about four kicks for each arm cycle.

The main thing to keep in mind as you're practicing this stroke, however, is to control the roll of your body as you swim. The nature of the backstroke is such that there is no way you can keep your body absolutely flat as you swim. Your shoulder has to dip into the water on each stroke, and each dip will cause your body to roll somewhat. That's okay, as long as your body doesn't pitch so much from side to side that your body "rolls" and is interfering with your progress in the water. Concentrate on the proper arm and leg movements and let the roll take care of itself.

A Safety Tip

A note of caution: the backstroke carries one hazard that isn't a problem in other strokes—you stand a good chance of bumping your head if you don't keep track of where you are in the pool. Some people solve this problem by counting the number of strokes needed to swim a lap, but I usually fix on something outside the pool—a beach chair or something on the wall—that tells me I'm close to the wall and count the strokes from this point. The point, in any case, is to be careful, and if you feel you're close to the wall, keep one hand behind you and propel yourself with your feet only. You may not go as fast, but you won't leave the pool with a bump on your head, either.

Breaststroke

Because your body stays in its most natural floating position in the breaststroke, it's probably the least complicated and the least strenuous of all the basic strokes, but don't sell its fitness benefit short. The breaststroke does a better job of firming the muscles in your inner and outer thighs than do the other basic strokes, and because it allows you to keep your eyes in front of you at all times, it's the one stroke you may have to use more than any other if you swim in a crowded pool.

Body Position

The starting position for the breaststroke is streamlined and prone. Your legs should be straight and together, your toes pointed outward. Your arms are in front of you, with palms facing down. The only parts of your body that are out of the water are your heels and your buttocks.

Kick

There are several different kicks you can do with the breaststroke. If you learned to swim more than twenty years ago, chances are you use the so-called frog kick—that is, you start by separating your legs and continue by bringing them to your chest and then thrusting them outward again in a V shape before bringing them together as you glide.

There's nothing at all wrong with this kick, except that it's a little outdated. Most accomplished swimmers today use the whip-action kick, and competitive swimmers who do the butterfly use the dolphin kick, which I'll go into later in the chapter.

The main difference between the whip-action kick and the familiar frog kick is that your legs stay much closer together as you're drawing them to your chest, and you separate them only slightly as your heels are about to touch your buttocks. At this point, you turn your ankles outward and begin your thrust backward, separating your legs naturally as you drive your upper legs toward the surface of the water. The kick ends with the feet close together and flexed outward.

The Arm Pull

Arm action on the breaststroke shouldn't give you too much trouble since it's a fairly basic motion. It's simply a wide, arclike pulling movement in which there are only two fundamentals you need to focus on: (1) a high elbow position, and (2) a shifting hand position, depending upon where you happen to be in the stroke.

The movement begins with your arms stretched straight in front of you. The initial phase of the movement involves nothing more complicated than simply parting the water in as wide a circular movement as you can comfortably manage. Once your arms are stretched out to the side, your hands rotate slightly so that the palms are now facing each other. Then you simply shoot your arms straight in front of you to the starting position, where you hold it for a few seconds.

This sequence illustrates the arm pull on the breaststroke. Notice the position of the hands in photo B: at this point your palms are against the surface of the water. Later in the stroke however (D), your hands turn toward each other.

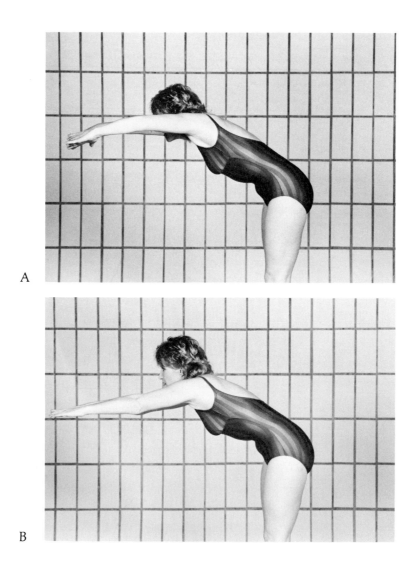

A

B

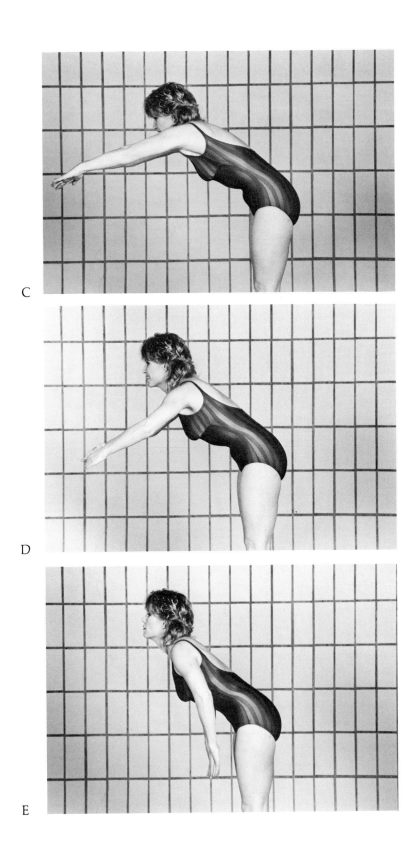

C

D

E

Breathing

Some swimmers like to keep their heads out of the water throughout the breaststroke. I don't swim this way because it puts added strain on the neck muscles and makes the breaststroke harder than it needs to be. Besides, putting your head in the water not only allows you to swim in a more relaxed manner, it also helps you coordinate the various movements of the stroke.

The only tricky part of the breathing during the breaststroke is that you don't inhale until you're about halfway through the first phase of the arm pull, at just about the time when your arms are at their widest point. At this point your head should be out of the water just long enough to take in air. The exhale begins after the glide and just as you're *beginning* the pull.

Putting It All Together

The sequence of movements that leads to a smooth breaststroke can be broken down into four basic components: the arm pull, the leg recovery, the leg thrust, and the glide.

1. The arm pull.

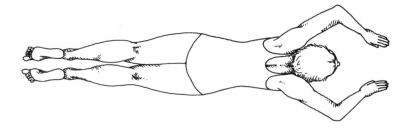

With your legs extended and your head *in* the water, begin the arm pull, exhaling as you lift your head from the water. (Your legs at this point do nothing.)

2. Leg recovery.

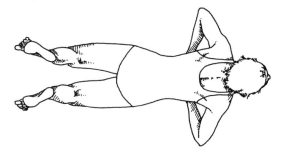

As you reach the end of the pull, with your head out of the water (you're now inhaling), bring your legs forward by flexing your knees and hips.

3. Leg thrust.

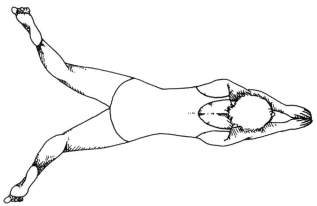

The leg thrust begins as your arms are beginning to finish the arclike movement. Your face is completely in the water at that point.

4. The glide.

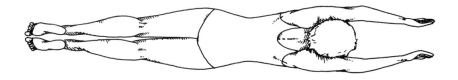

The glide should continue to at least a count of three. Your body is fully extended, your head is still in the water, and you are exhaling.

The Butterfly Stroke

The butterfly is probably the most difficult of the basic strokes; that's because it requires the most muscle strength and the most precise coordination. Then again, the only stroke faster than the butterfly is the freestyle, and the times for the butterfly have been improving so rapidly over the years that many people think that it will eventually surpass the freestyle.

The butterfly is built around many of the same principles we've already covered in the other strokes. The only major difference is in the kick and the arm pull, so let's look at some of the fundamentals.

Body Position

As in the freestyle and conventional breaststroke, a streamlined body position is essential. To assure this position, try to keep your head fairly low and your elbows high, and pay particularly close attention to your kick.

Kick

The dolphin kick is probably the hardest kick to learn, but once you've mastered it, it's a lot of fun and will generate more speed than any other kick.

As the name implies, the dolphin kick is nothing more than a quick, flicking kick in which your legs kick together as one. Start with your feet positioned the way you would if you were doing the whip-action kick. The difference, however, is that instead of spreading your legs outward, you keep them fairly close together (not pressed tightly together) and kick backward with both feet at the same time. The best way to envision this is to think of it as a two-footed hop in the water.

There are actually two kicks in the dolphin kick: a down kick and an up kick. The first comes when your head is down and your arms are first beginning their pull. The second comes during the glide portion of the stroke.

Let me warn you ahead of time about this kick. In addition to the flexible ankles I already talked about, the dolphin kick takes strong legs and strong stomach muscles to do well. Then again, practicing the stroke helps you develop and firm those muscles. The more you do it, the stronger you'll become.

Without question the best way to learn this kick is to practice with a kickboard. Make sure you keep the board flat, and try to keep it relatively still as you're kicking.

The Arm Pull

The arm pull in the butterfly is sometimes called an hourglass movement and other times an S pull. Whatever you call it, the thing to keep in mind is that it isn't all that different from the basic crawl movement. The only real difference is that when you are doing the butterfly, both arms are moving *simultaneously*.

There are several different breathing patterns you can use when you're doing the butterfly stroke. Some competitive swimmers like to breathe every three strokes; others prefer an every-two-stroke pattern. You can vary it even more, taking a breath after the first two strokes, then after one stroke, and again after two strokes, and so on. It all depends on how fast and how far you want to swim. The shorter the distance and the faster you want to swim, the fewer breaths you want to take during the course of the distance.

Whichever pattern you choose, the mechanics stay the same. You need to time your inhale to begin with the last part of the arm pull and your exhale—in the water—as your hands and shoulders reach about shoulder level.

Putting It All Together

Because your objectives in the butterfly stroke are power and speed, timing your kick to your arm pull is probably more critical than it is for other strokes. The top butterfly swimmers use a two-kick-for-one-arm-cycle pattern, timing the first kick to begin as soon as the arms enter the water and timing the downward beat of the second as soon as the pull is about halfway finished and your arms are just coming out of the water.

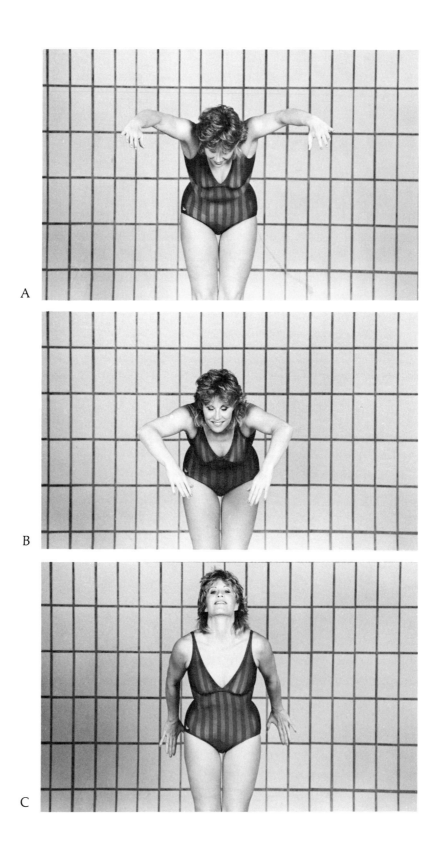

A

B

C

D

This is a front view of the butterfly pull. Notice that my arms are about 45 degrees away from my body when I would enter the water (A) but move toward each other (B) as they cut downward through the water.

Sidestroke

Nobody swims the sidestroke competitively anymore, and it's not the best stroke to work on if you're swimming for fitness. But it's certainly good to know how to do because it's probably the most relaxing of all the various swimming strokes—for this reason it's a good stroke for cooling down—and the one stroke that enables you to see where you're going at all times, which is why it is emphasized in lifesaving instruction.

Body Position

That you swim this stroke in a horizontal side position doesn't mean that streamlining is any less important than it is for other strokes. Your body should be flat in the water and your neck should be raised only slightly—just enough so that you can breathe through your mouth.

The Kick

The kick for the sidestroke is a basic scissors kick. You begin from a legs-extended position by bringing your heels toward your hips so that you're in a semifetal position. From this position you make a large scissors motion, with your top leg moving forward and your bottom leg moving backward. You then bring them together again and straighten before repeating the movement.

There's one variation on this kick: It's simply a reverse scissors kick, in which your bottom leg moves forward and your top leg moves backward:

The Variation

The Arm Motion

The arm motion for the sidestroke is simpler to do than to explain. The best way to envision it is to pretend you're sleeping on your side, with your bottom arm extended straight above you and the other comfortably at your side. That's the glide position. What happens during the actual stroke is that the extended arm pulls downward while the other hand simply bends at the elbow. The two arms meet at roughly chest level. Then, while the bottom arm is moving back to its original position, the top arm is pulling straight back to its original position.

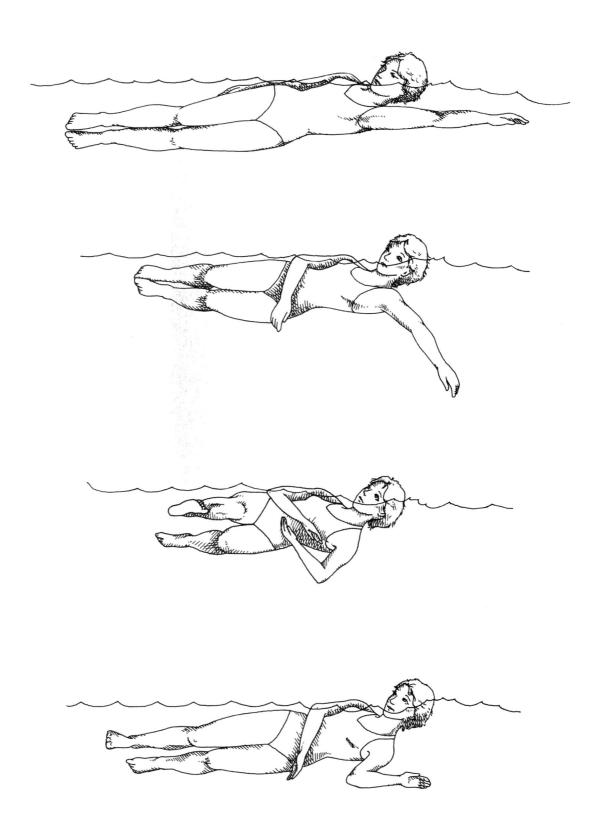

Breathing

The breathing on the sidestroke should be timed to the speed of the stroke. You inhale as you begin the first phase of the pull and you exhale just as your bottom arm is beginning to recover. You continue to exhale throughout the glide.

Putting It All Together

Timing is not too difficult for the sidestroke, since your arm and leg movements are naturally coordinated. You start the bottom arm pull at the same time that you're lifting your knees to begin the scissors kick, and you time the extension of your legs to begin with the pull of the upper leg. You then hold this position for the glide.

Turns

Being able to turn properly isn't as important when you're swimming for fitness as it is when you're swimming for speed, but it's still an important skill to learn. For one thing, if you don't know how to turn, you could hurt yourself when you're swimming certain strokes, the backstroke in particular. And if you don't turn properly, you'll have trouble establishing a smooth rhythm when you're swimming laps. Each time you come to the end of the pool, you'll have to interrupt your stroke and start over again.

There are essentially two types of turns: the so-called open turn, a variation of which is known as the closed turn, and the more advanced flip turn. You can get along very nicely without knowing the flip turn, but we'll look at both types anyway.

The Open Turn

The open turn is the most basic turn and the one you need to master first, before you graduate to the more advanced turns. You can use this turn for all strokes.

1. The approach.

The approach phase begins when you're roughly a stroke or two away from the end of the pool. At this point, you try to time your stroke so that one of your hands (it doesn't matter which) can reach out and grasp the gutters.

2. The turn.

Once you've grasped the gutter—or anchored your hand against the pool wall—you now tuck your legs in and swing your body around on the *same* side as the extended arm. Your head and body should remain close to the wall, and you should flex your elbow just slightly. Your free arm, in the meantime, should be extended in the direction from which you've come. Once you've rotated your legs so that they're against the wall, lift your head slightly and inhale. This is the actual turn segment.

3. The push-off.

You're now ready to push off. The arm that's been against the pool wall now swings over your shoulder and shoots out to join the arm that's already extended. At this point, your body is more sideways than prone, but your legs are flexed and against the wall and your head is tucked into your chest. You push off forcefully and assume the streamlined position as you glide.

The Backstroke Open Turn

The backstroke open turn is similar to the turn we've just talked about, the only difference being that you do it all on your back.

1. The approach.

The most important consideration for the approach is to time your last stroke so that you're not too close to the edge of the pool.

2. The turn.

Once you've grasped the gutter, bring your knees to your chest and rotate your body all the way around so that you're now facing the wall with your feet.

3. The push-off.

Your knees should bend when you plant your feet against the edge, so that you generate power on the push-off.

The Flip Turn

The flip turn involves a somersault movement and is a good deal more difficult to execute than the open turn. It's not an easy turn to master, but it's impressive once you've learned how to do it. Here are the steps.

1. The approach.

The main thing to keep in mind is to maintain your speed. Your turn should begin when you're about four feet from the wall.

2. The flip.

The power behind the flip comes from your legs and involves a movement similar to the dolphin kick we talked about earlier when we described the butterfly stroke. While you are making this kick, shoot both hands downward.

3. Pulling through the flip.

The combination of the kick and your hands shooting downward should give you enough momentum to bring your hips out of the water, but you have to provide the rest of the power with your hands by pushing hard directly downward. This hand pushing against the water should be enough to hurtle your feet out of the water.

4. The twist.

In order to keep yourself from landing on your back, you need to twist your body sideways (I told you the move was complicated) and to pull your right arm around in a small circle.

5. The push-off.

If you've done the flip properly, you should be ready to plant your feet against the wall when you're about halfway through the flip. You then continue to roll over until you're facedown in the water, at which time you use your feet to push yourself off.

Diving

I was a competitive diver before I was a competitive swimmer, and even though I wasn't very good at it (which is why I became a competitive swimmer), I always enjoyed diving—and still do. Diving is *fun*. While I don't expect you to incorporate any high-platform diving into your Hydro-Aerobics, it's still nice to know how to dive smoothly and gracefully from the side of the pool (and essential, if you ever intend to race).

Whether you are diving from the side of the pool or from a high platform, the basics remain pretty much the same—two of which are very important. One is achieving the streamlined position I've been talking about throughout this chapter (which means avoiding the temptation to raise your head too soon). The other is keeping your body as *tight* as possible during the dive itself.

If you keep these two points in mind and follow the sequence I've set up for you in this section, you should have little or no trouble learning a very serviceable dive.

The Sitting Dive

If you have never dived before, you should take your first practice dives from a sitting position. Here are the steps.

1. The starting position.

Sit on the edge of the pool with your heels flat against the wall. (If you can curl your toes around the edge of a gutter for extra support, so much the better.) Now extend your arms straight in front of you, keeping your head in between your upper arms and locking your hands together with your thumbs. Now, pull your arms and head down until your chin is resting on your chest and point your hands downward toward the water.

2. The push-off and entry.

Bend forward from the waist and simply push (really push!) your heels away from the gutter, while extending your legs and body vigorously. If you do this move correctly, you'll enter the water in a streamlined position (like a plank), with your head down. Time your exhale just before the entry.

3. Resurfacing.

To resurface, you don't change your body position all that much. Simply glide for a while, then arch your back and point your fingers upward to guide your ascent. If you want to hasten the ascent, do a quick flutter kick.

The Kneeling Dive

Once you've mastered the sitting dive, you're ready for the next step—the *kneeling dive*. Once again, the same principles apply: your body must enter the water in as tight and streamlined a position as possible.

1. The starting position.

Assume a kneeling position, with one knee touching the ground and the toes of the other leg wrapped around the edge of the pool. Then, as you did on the sitting dive, extend your arms in front of you, tuck your chin into your chest, and bend at the waist.

2. Takeoff and entry.

Holding your kneeling position, raise slightly and lean forward. (To keep from falling into the water, you'll have to shift your weight gradually from the back foot to the front foot.) Now for the tricky part: with your weight still on the front foot and your head down, raise your hips by straightening your back leg. Continue to straighten the leg until you can no longer maintain your balance and push off with the *front* foot, bringing your legs together as you enter the water. Keep your body stiff as you enter the water, with your hands pointed downward. Again, try to time your exhale just prior to entry.

3. Resurfacing.

The resurfacing movement from the kneeling dive is no different from the resurfacing movement from the sitting dive. You glide in the streamlined position, arch your back slightly, and point your fingers upward.

Standing Dive

Some instructors precede the standing dive with the semi-standing dive (sometimes known as the "stork position"), but if you are able to do the kneeling dive, chances are you can go directly to the standing dive without much trouble.

1. The starting position.

Stand at the edge of the pool and assume the "pike" position. Your arms are extended, you are bending at the waist, and your knees are slightly bent.

The key to the takeoff is to *spring* up from the edge of the pool, rather than simply "fall" into the water. Once you're airborne, the idea is to straighten your legs behind you so that your body is straight and no longer piked. If you're not an experienced diver, you'll probably have trouble straightening your body while you're in flight and enter the water with your body still somewhat piked. Stick with it, though. If you concentrate on straightening your body as soon as you've pushed off, you'll get the hang of it sooner than you might expect.

3. Entry and resurfacing.

If you push off with enough spring and achieve the proper body position on the dive, you can then relax and enjoy the ride. Hold your position throughout the glide (exhaling slowly) and resurface as you've been doing all along, by arching your back and extending your fingers upward. Keep in mind that the higher the dive, the faster you'll hit the water and the longer you'll glide.

Racing Dives

The difference between a racing dive and a normal dive is that when you race, you want to achieve *length*, not height, and you want the dive to propel you as far forward as possible. There are two basic racing dives: (1) the wind-up dive, in which you use a windmill-like motion with your arms to generate more forward movement; and (2) the grab start, in which you take hold of the edge of the pool and use the leverage to propel you forward.

The Wind-up Dive

1. The starting position.

In competitive swimming, you line up on a starting block about thirty inches above the surface of the water. Your pool may not have starting blocks, so let's assume you're lining up at the pool's edge. You should be in a slightly piked position with your knees slightly bent and your arms hanging loosely at your side.

2. The wind-up.

Just before you're ready to push off, shoot your arms forward until they reach shoulder level (which will propel your body forward) and then sweep forward, outward and upward until they are alongside your knees.

3. Takeoff and entry.

Once your arms have reached your knees, push off by straightening your knees and continue the forward arm movement until your arms are extended in front of you, fingers extended. Lift your head slightly, but keep your legs as straight as possible and try to enter the water with as little angle as possible. Hold that position briefly and then start to kick and pull at the same time.

The Grab Start

The chief advantage the grab start has over the windmill start is that it gets you into the water a little sooner. Here's how it looks:

1. The starting position.

Line up as you would for any dive, but this time reach forward and grasp the gutter (in a race, you would grab the front edge of the starting block).

2. Takeoff and entry.

Start the takeoff by using your hands to pull yourself forward. Release your hold and throw your arms forward as your legs straighten during the push-off. Again, the idea is to land as shallow as possible, with your body streamlined.

6· How to Get Ready

E nough preliminaries. You now know the philosophy behind Hydro-Aerobics, you know the routines, and you know something about the basics of good swimming. Let's focus on the Hydro-Aerobics workouts themselves: how to organize them, how to go through them, and how to get the most out of them.

Finding a Good Place to Work Out

I wish I could tell you that it's as easy to find a good place to do your Hydro-Aerobics workouts as it is to find a good place to run, but anybody who has done both—like me—knows that I'd be lying.

The basic problem isn't finding a place to work out—it's finding the right swimming environment. True, when you're in the water, the environment tends to be the same no matter where you're swimming, but the attractiveness of the pool itself, not to mention the locker facilities, can vary from the ultraluxurious to the ultradepressing, and the water itself—how cold or chlorinated or choppy it is—can vary enormously from pool to pool. And while these nonswimming considerations will have little bearing on the purely physical benefits that swimming itself will bring you, they do affect the *totality* of the swimming experience, and I don't think you should ignore them.

What I'm suggesting, then, is that if you don't already have a place to work out that you look forward to going to, you take the time to find not just *any* place but the best possible place, given your particular needs: your schedule, your comfort demands, your personality. I can assure you one thing: The more pleasing the entire swimming experience, the more you're going to get out of the swimming itself.

The Location

The pool in which you intend to do most of your working out should be close enough to where you live or work so that you can get to it in a reasonable amount of time and without too much hassle. Most of us have busy schedules, and if simply getting to and from the pool (not counting the time it takes you to change into and out of your suit) adds much more than twenty-five or thirty minutes to the overall time you spend swimming, chances are you're going to have trouble maintaining a regular schedule. Yes, in the beginning, when you're highly motivated, you might not care about that extra half-hour or so, but as time goes on, you can safely assume that the less convenient the location of the pool, the more likely the possibility that you'll find reasons for not going: you're too busy, you don't feel like making the drive (or taking a taxi, bus, or subway), the weather is lousy, and so on.

Ideally (and I know we can't always expect the ideal), the pool you work out in shouldn't be any more than a ten-minute drive, walk, or bike ride from your home or place of business. Such a pool shouldn't be tough to find. If you're fortunate, you might live in an apartment or condominium complex that has its own pool, or you might live near an apartment or hotel that has an indoor pool and offers reasonably priced pool memberships. (Interestingly enough, many people find it easier to swim when they travel than when they stay at home. That's because most good hotels and motels these days have either a pool or access to a pool.) Most Ys and health clubs with pools are located convenient to downtown business areas, and there's a good chance there's a pool somewhere between your home and your place of work, which means that you can stop there on your way either to or from work.

The Size

You don't need an Olympic-size pool to get an Olympic-size Hydro-Aerobics workout. I've had terrific workouts in pools that were no more than 25 feet long. More important than the size, to my mind, is how crowded the pool gets. I'd much rather swim in a smaller pool with fewer people than in a championship-size pool with too many people.

The Water

Don't be apologetic if you're choosy about the water in the pool you swim in. I don't enjoy swimming in a pool in which the water is too cold or too chlorinated, and these days, with more and more pools opening throughout the country, you don't have to put up with being too cold or having your eyes burn just for the sake of staying fit. Pools are no different from other athletic facilities. Some are well built; some aren't. Some pools have poor filtering systems, which is why they have to add so much chlorine to the water, or have badly built gutter systems, which makes the water choppy. It's hard to tell just how choppy the water is if there isn't anybody in the pool, and that's why when you're visiting a pool with the idea of taking out a membership, you should try to go at the peak hours (or at least during the hours you expect to be swimming normally).

The Atmosphere

What I've just said about the water in a pool goes for the overall atmosphere as well. Keep in mind what I said at the start of this book: Swimming should be a *pleasant* experience, and the pleasantness of the experience shouldn't be confined to the swimming only. The locker rooms should be clean and comfortable, and the pool area itself should be nicely lit and attractive. (Nothing depresses me more than to go into a pool in which half the bulbs are out of commission and the paint is peeling.) In other words, the pool itself, quite apart from what happens inside it, should be an inviting place in its own right: you should look forward to going there.

Part of the atmosphere, too, has to do with the people you meet when you swim. Because I'm biased (as you already know), I find most people who swim to be nice people, but in some clubs, there are swimming cliques—people who've been swimming there for years and who aren't pleased when somebody new comes aboard. (For one thing, it means another body in the water.) You should be able to get a good fix on the atmosphere

Swimmer's Etiquette

As with most sports—tennis, for instance—there is an etiquette to swimming, a number of rules that have grown up through the years and that swimmers throughout the world simply expect to be obeyed. Here are the most important:

1. Learn the local rules.

Before you work out at any club or pool for the first time, ask either a member or the lifeguard to explain the local system. Find out, for instance, on which side of the lane you swim when you're going one way and which side when you're going the other way.

2. Stay in your assigned lane.

One of the things you're going to have to learn if you're going to swim laps in a pool that caters to serious swimmers is to swim in a straight line. At most pools, there are lines that divide each lane into two areas, and you'll be expected to swim to the right of each line within those boundaries.

3. Keep out of the way of other swimmers.

If you're working on exercises or swimming very slowly, try to find a part of the pool (if possible) in which your workout won't interfere with swimmers who are only doing laps. In most clubs,

in a club fairly easily. Talk to the pro and see how friendly (or aloof) he or she is. Chat with the attendants (if there are any), and take notice of whether the swimmers are doing anything to make you feel welcome or are going out of their way to ignore you. Mind you, I'm not suggesting that you join a club purely for the social aspect of swimming, but it's important to feel comfortable with the people you're with, even if the only time you get to see them is when you're swimming.

there are sections set aside for the kind of exercises you'll be doing. Otherwise you may have to plan your workout for a time when the lanes aren't as crowded.

4. Respect the time limit.

At some pools, during the busiest periods, you're assigned a lane for a specified period of time—sometimes no more than 20 minutes. If this is the case, you may have no choice but to break your workout into two parts. Doing so, of course, will add more time to your workouts, but don't worry about the fitness effect. Breaking up the workout will have little or no effect on its benefits.

5. Be courteous to slower—or faster—swimmers.

Most pools have specially designated areas in the lanes for passing, but you still need to look for other swimmers whether you're passing or *being* passed. If you sense that a swimmer in your lane is swimming at a faster pace than you (and you can usually tell this whenever you're turning), either wait at the wall until the faster swimmer has made his or her turn and pushed off or else try to swim closer to the side wall on the next lap so that you give the faster swimmer room to pass. And if *you're* doing the passing, make sure you check whether someone is about to move into the lane from the opposite direction.

The Program and Schedule

A good swimming facility will have a balanced program: not only regularly scheduled instructional water aerobics programs and, in the case of pools, a team program, but enough open swim time so that if you want to do your own workouts, you won't have to do them at a strange hour when nobody else is swimming. True, you may not find an *ideal* situation, but take the time to find a club that will allow you to carry out your workouts without a constant hassle.

Making Your Workouts More Enjoyable

Years ago, when I first began swimming competitively, you used to show up at the pool with nothing but your bathing suit, a towel, and maybe a bathing cap. But go to any swimming training center today and you'll be amazed by the amount of equipment many swimmers now take with them. Some purists are critical of this new trend, but I disagree. As I see it, as long as a piece of equipment can make swimming more pleasant and easier for you, why not use it—just as long as it isn't too expensive or too cumbersome to carry with you.

Let me stress here that none of the swimming aids I'm going to be talking about in this chapter is *essential* in order for you to do the Hydro-Aerobics workouts. But many of them will make the workouts more enjoyable, so give them some thought.

Goggles: A New Essential

Goggles are all but indispensable if you are going to swim with any regularity. Their most obvious benefit is that they keep the chlorine in the water from irritating your eyes (and if you wear contacts, by the way, you have no choice: you *have* to use goggles). A less obvious but just as important benefit is that wearing goggles enables you to keep your eyes open in the water, which, as we'll see later, becomes an important efficiency factor when you're swimming.

There are any number of different makes of goggles on the market and they come in a variety of tints, from clear to green and blue and gray. Goggles today are a lot more expensive than they used to be, but you can buy a serviceable pair for $5 or less, and it's not a bad idea to buy several pairs with different tints, just for the sake of variety. If you wear glasses, you can order prescription goggles, but they can be as much as ten times as expensive as regular goggles, and I'm not sure you really need them.

But whatever the tint or prescription, the important thing to bear in mind about goggles is make sure they fit and are comfortable, for nothing is more distracting when you swim than to have the goggles slip and water pour into your eyes. To make sure of the fit, you'll probably have to go to a swimming goods store and try on several different kinds simply to see which feels the best over your eyes. Goggles should fit snugly, but you don't want them so tight that they leave an indentation in your skin when you take them off. Remember, too, that if you're going to wear a bathing cap when you swim, make sure you wear the cap when you're trying on the goggles.

Depending upon how often you swim, a good pair of goggles should last from six months to a year. After that, the rubber begins to stretch or wear out and the goggles lose their watertightness. As far as caring for the goggles goes, the only ongoing problem you'll run into is lens fogging. There are some preparations you can buy in most swim-goods stores that help prevent this fogging, but I find that if I simply dip the goggles in the water before I put them on, it pretty much solves the problem. Keep it simple.

Fins: Not Just for Kids and Scuba Divers

A few years ago, I was staying at a hotel in Florida that had a lovely pool, and one morning as I was getting ready for my workout, a man arrived at the pool carrying a pair of swim fins. There were a handful of other swimmers in the pool who apparently knew each other, and I couldn't help but notice that they were chuckling to themselves, obviously amused by the image of a man sitting at the edge of a swimming pool putting on a pair of swimming fins.

Well, they didn't chuckle long. Far from being the novice swimmer the onlookers might have taken him for, the man turned out to be a former collegiate swimmer, and his smooth, powerful strokes quickly turned the chuckles into nervous smiles of admiration.

And what was a former collegiate swimmer doing with a pair of swim fins? Very simply, what a lot of former and even current championship swimmers do with them: He used them regularly as part of his workouts. *He* knew, if the swimmers who were at first amused didn't, that swim fins can help your workouts in a number of ways.

First of all, as Bob Horn likes to emphasize to all his students, fins help you swim more easily and more efficiently. With the exception of only one stroke—the breaststroke (the only stroke you can't swim with fins)—fins not only propel you through the water more easily, they help to stabilize your body position: They keep your body from dipping too low in the water. This benefit is important for all strokes, but particularly for the backstroke, when being too low in the water means that you're constantly having to suck the water away from your nose.

But just as important, swim fins take some of the stress away from your arms and put it where it can do the most good: on the largest muscles in your body—your leg muscles. This transfer of stress means your arms and shoulders won't become as tired or as tight as they often do for swimmers who have a tendency (as most do) to drag their legs and rely mainly on their arms and shoulders to power the stroke. So, with your arms not becoming as tired, you can swim for longer periods of time and derive the added cardiovascular benefits of distance swimming. In fact, one of the best cardiovascular workouts you can do is to use fins with a kickboard.

Yet another benefit that fins bring you is that they help you make turns more smoothly. The key to an efficient turn, remember, is building momentum just prior to reaching the edge of the pool, and it's much easier to build this momentum with fins than without them.

Finally, fins add a weight-training dimension to your workout. Wearing fins increases the resistance your legs will encounter with each kick, and this resistance will translate into more strength.

There are quite a few fins on the market today, ranging in price anywhere from $20 to $40. I go along with Bob Horn, who recommends the Churchill Fins. They cost more—about $40—but they'll last you a lifetime. The problem with cheaper fins is that it's tough to get a good fit, and you sometimes end up spending more time adjusting your fins than you do swimming.

Bathing Caps: More Than Cosmetic

Whether you're a woman or a man, it makes sense to swim with a cap, but not the kind you buy in a drugstore and not to keep your hair dry. The kind of caps most serious swimmers wear don't keep hair dry. The latex or Lycra caps that the top swimmers use keep water from flowing out of their hair and onto their face. And if you're a man who's a little bald on top and you intend to swim outdoors, a bathing cap can protect the top of your head from sunburn. The best place to buy a good bathing cap, by the way, is not in a drugstore but in a swimming goods store.

Earplugs and Nose Clips: Make Sure You Really Need Them

Special plugs for your ears and clips for your nose are inexpensive and would seem to be excellent aids for swimmers, but unless you have a specific medical reason for wearing them—a serious sinus condition, for instance, or a serious ear problem—I would pass.

The problem with nose plugs (apart from the fact that they can be very uncomfortable) is that they don't give you a chance to exhale properly. As you'll see later when we talk about breathing, you never use your nose when you're *inhaling,* but you should exhale through both your mouth *and* your nose.

My reservations about earplugs stem from my own experience with them: that it's next to impossible to find a pair that really works—a pair, that is, that will really keep the water out of your ears. Worse, the simple act of inserting and taking out earplugs can sometimes cause an inflammation.

But these are *my* feelings. I know swimmers who wear earplugs and nose clips and recommend them enthusiastically.

Suiting Up

The best advice I can give you about bathing suits is to keep them simple and sturdy. The most practical suits for men and women alike are racing suits, made of either nylon or a blend of nylon and Lycra. What's nice about these suits is that they are lightweight, they hold their color well, and they dry fast.

Kickboards and Other Aids

A kickboard is nothing more than a thin slab of plastic or Styrofoam that floats and enables you to practice your kicking. Because I think a kickboard is a very useful aid (I'd much rather practice my kick using one than holding on to the side of the pool, which, to me, is like running in place), I have included a few kickboard routines in the Hydro-Aerobics program. These routines are optional, which means you don't *have* to buy a kickboard, but using one will add variety to your workout and give you the opportunity to improve your kicking technique.

Some instructors like to see their students practice their kicking by holding on to the side of the pool, but most people (including me) find kicking that way terribly boring. I'd rather see you use a wood or Styrofoam kickboard.

There are several ways of using a kickboard. One is to hold the board with your hands outstretched in front of you, which will give you room to put your face in the water and practice breathing. Another is to lie with your arms on top of the board, with your fingers holding on to the board's front edge. Whichever method you use, the important thing is to stay relaxed (particularly at your ankles).

The things you need to be aware of *as* you're kicking are the following:

- Body position—keep it horizontal.
- Knees—only slightly bent.
- Hip involvement—use the entire leg.
- Depth—keep your legs *in* the water: Only the heels should break the surface.

A

C

B

Here are three different ways to position yourself on the kickboard. In photo A, I'm holding on to the end of it. In photo B, I'm grasping it about midway, and in photo C, I've taken hold of the front. There is no "right" way to hold a kickboard. It's simply a matter of what feels best for you.

Another aid worth looking into (and I've tried to limit the amount of Hydro-Aerobics workouts that call for these aids) are so-called inflatable floaties. These devices are popular among people who do water ballet exercises, but the exercises I recommend with them are intended mainly to develop strength and tone.

There aren't too many items I can add to this list of swimming aids other than a few obvious things: a nice towel, a comfortable bathing suit, and a mesh bag to carry all this equipment in. So let's turn now to yet another important—and overlooked—aspect of the swimming experience: working it into your lifestyle.

Making Swimming a Priority

I don't mean to sound preachy, but to get the most out of swimming, you need to make it a priority in your life, and this means setting aside the time. The programs I've set up for you later in the book are based on a three-times-per-week schedule. The sky isn't going to fall if you have to miss a workout now and then, but it's important that you maintain a reasonably regular schedule of workouts. Exercise does the most for you when you make it a habit.

If possible, and if your schedule allows, try to arrange your time so that you're working at more or less the same hour each day: during the early morning, at noon, or after work. If I were to choose the *best* time to work out, I would say early morning, even if you live in a cold climate and the thought of diving into a pool when it's still dark and cold outside strikes you as barbaric. Granted, it may take you a while to get into the routine of early-morning swimming, but an early-morning workout sets you up for the rest of the day. When I am able to start my day with a morning workout, I not only feel better physically the rest of the day, but I feel sharper mentally as well. I know I've done something good for my body, and I'm pleased by the fact that I've started my day by accomplishing something.

If you're lucky enough to have a flexible schedule—you have your own business, say, or you free-lance—you have an advantage over most people. You can build your schedule around the times when other people are working and the pool is relatively quiet. Here again, however, the same principle holds: Try to set your workouts at more or less the same time every day. The more routinized you become in your approach to swimming, the easier it's going to be for you to maintain a regular schedule of workouts.

One more point about scheduling, and it may be the most important of all: Don't cram swimming into your schedule. If you have to rush to get to the pool, rush to change, rush to shower afterward, and rush back to work, whatever physical benefit you derive from the workout will be more than offset by the mental stress you've undergone. Your Hydro-Aerobics workout should begin not when you first enter the water but when you leave your house or your job and are on your way to the pool. That's when you can shift into a lower, more relaxed gear, because now you're doing something for *you*, something that's yours alone. Savor those minutes. Give your brain a rest. Listen to good music—I know some swimmers who even refuse to listen to the news when they're on their way to a pool because they don't want to hear anything that might depress them—or, if you're with a swimming friend, keep the conversation light.

And while I'm on the subject, it's not a bad idea to find yourself a swimming companion. It's not essential, and if the person isn't as committed to swimming as you are, it could end up interfering with your schedule. But having somebody whose company you enjoy to drive or walk with you to the pool—even if the two of you work out separately—simply adds another positive element to the overall experience.

7· THE HYDRO-AEROBICS WORKOUTS

Apart from whatever fitness goals you may establish for yourself, there are two important factors to consider before you begin working with the Hydro-Aerobics exercises that appear later in this chapter. The first is your current level of swimming ability—in particular, how long a period you can swim without stopping; the second is your current level of fitness. The two aren't necessarily related. You may be in good enough aerobic shape to *run* five miles, but in the water, you could be winded after only two laps. Why? Two reasons. First, swimming involves muscles you don't use when you run. And second, if you don't breathe properly when you swim, it doesn't matter what kind of shape you're in—you're going to be winded after only a minute or two.

Another thing: if you haven't done any vigorous exercising, make sure you check with your physician before you start.

The Workouts: How Frequently, How Long

The question of how frequently you work out and how long each of the workouts should be is troublesome no matter what the fitness activity may be, and swimming is no exception. The basic problem is finding that balance between what is physically beneficial and what is practical and convenient for you. Most exercise experts—Kenneth Cooper in particular—now agree that you don't have to work out every day in order to stay fit, and some programs—the Nautilus program, for instance—are meant to be followed on no more than a three-day-a-week basis.

133

The principle at work here is the ratio of benefit to effort. Studies by Cooper and others have established that you can achieve a superior level of cardiovascular fitness if you manage to swim continuously, at a reasonably fast pace, for at least 20 minutes three or four times a week. Many swimmers, of course, swim for longer periods of time and at a greater frequency per week, but most studies show that once you reach a certain threshold, the added time you spend swimming during each workout or any increase in the number of times you work out per week doesn't produce a *corresponding* cardiovascular benefit.

This is not to say that there aren't other benefits beyond aerobic fitness that come from increasing the number and the intensity of your workouts. Obviously the more you exercise, the more calories you burn, and working out every day could well serve an important psychological function for you: You may simply *feel* better, physically and mentally, when you work out every day. But if you're going to get involved with any fitness program, it's important that you understand the physiological dynamics of it and that you recognize what physiological benefits you are—and aren't—getting in relation to the time and effort you put in.

The workouts I've set up for you in this book range from 30 minutes to 45 minutes each. I've set up this range deliberately, so that you can tailor workouts to fit your own schedule. Ideally, you should work out for at least 30 minutes, with at least 20 minutes devoted to aerobic exercise, but I've gone through very busy weeks during which I've worked out for only 20 minutes, and I haven't noticed any *major* change in my level of fitness. The point is, you have more flexibility than you may think when you're involved in a fitness program, and there are too many variables (including your own psychology) to say that *one* program at *one* length and at *one* frequency per week will meet everybody's needs.

Working with Target Pulse Rate

A second factor that will determine how you plan your workouts involves your current level of aerobic fitness, which is usually measured in terms of your ability to exercise over a prolonged period of time, no matter what the activity.

The best measuring stick involves a principle known as the training effect or, as it is sometimes referred to, your target pulse rate.

In order to develop an optimum level of aerobic fitness, your cardiovascular system must receive a workout vigorous enough to produce beneficial changes. One of the most reliable ways to determine just how much of a workout your cardiovascular system is getting is to keep track of your pulse rate during the exercise. Studies by Dr. Cooper and others have determined that in order to achieve the so-called training effect, your pulse has to reach a certain point—the target pulse rate—and remain at that point for approximately 20 minutes.

A target pulse rate represents, roughly speaking, the number of times per minute you want your heart to be pumping for at least 20 minutes during the course of a 40-minute workout. Why 20 minutes? Because it's now generally agreed that it takes at least 15 minutes (Cooper says 20; others say less) of effort at the target pulse rate before the exercise can produce the physiological changes needed to enhance your aerobic fitness.

Just how consecutive and prolonged this minimum of 15 to 20 minutes has to be is still a matter of some debate. The researchers at the Aerobics Center in Dallas feel that for best results, the exercise that produces the target pulse rate should be *continuous,* but you have some flexibility here. Researchers at the center have discovered, for instance, that you can take intermittent breaks and still realize substantial aerobic fitness as long as two conditions are met: one, that the break interval is brief enough so that your pulse doesn't drop too low; and two, that the overall exercise is reasonably concentrated. In other words, 25 minutes of activity punctuated by a few brief breaks are probably as beneficial (or least nearly so) as 20 minutes of consecutive activity.

How to Determine Your Target Pulse Rate

The procedure for establishing your own target pulse rate is to first determine your so-called maximum heart rate—the rate at which your heart is capable of beating under conditions of extreme stress—when your heart is pumping oxygen to virtually all the muscles in the body. You do this, first of all, by subtracting your age from 220 if you're a man and 210 if you're a woman.

From here on in it gets a little complicated. Depending upon whom you talk to and what your fitness goals are, your target rate should be anywhere from 60 percent to 80 percent of that initial figure. As a general rule, the younger you are and the more fit you are, the higher the percentage you should use. So, if you are a thirty-five-year-old woman in reasonably good shape, you begin by subtracting 35 from 210, which would give you a starting figure of 175, and if you were to take 75 percent of that figure, you would end up with a target rate of about 132.

But there's yet another complication: the fact that the water, in and of itself, tends to lower your pulse rate. This means that whatever your target rate would be normally, you need to reduce it further—by about another 7 percent.

Are you totally confused? Let me try to simplify things for you. If your pulse is in the normal range—anywhere from 70 to 78—and you are between thirty-five and forty-five years old, you can pretty much figure on a target rate of about 120 when you swim. If your resting pulse is a little lower or a little higher, vary your target rate accordingly. Similarly, if you're older—or younger—than the ages I've listed, make the same kind of adjustments: Raise the target if you're younger, lower it if you're older.

If you want still another way to figure your target rate, try this: Subtract your resting pulse—the number of times per minute your heart is usually beating when you wake up in the morning—from your maximum heart rate; take 50 percent of that number and add it to your resting pulse. So if you have a resting pulse of 72, and your maximum heart rate, based on the formula I've already given you, was 180, your target rate would be about 126 ($180 - 72 = 108/2 = 54 + 72 = 126$).

Let me emphasize here that these numbers are approximate. Any number of factors can affect your own target rate, and it's not a bad idea to find a cardiovascular fitness center in your area so that you can be tested and have a target rate established for you.

Determining Your Current Level of Fitness

To determine your current level of Hydro-Aerobics fitness, you need first to determine how long you can swim the crawl, at maximum effort, without feeling strain or without getting winded. Your goal should be 20 minutes.

level 1: 5 minutes or less
level 2: between 5 and 11 minutes
level 3: between 12 and 19 minutes
level 4: 20 minutes or more

WARNING: If while you're doing this test, you experience any of the following symptoms, you should stop immediately and consult a doctor before doing any more exercising.

- any sharp pain, particularly in the chest or arm
- nausea
- unusually high or irregular heartbeat
- lightheadedness
- tremors or shakiness
- any unusual sensation you can't explain

How to Take Your Pulse

Probably the simplest way to take your pulse is to find the carotid artery (it's in your neck), count the number of times your pulse is beating in 6 seconds and add a zero. But more and more fitness specialists feel that 6 seconds is too short a time to give you an accurate count, especially since many people have irregular pulses. Variations on this procedure are to take the pulse for 10 seconds and multiply by 6 or take it for 15 seconds and multiply it by 4. Use whatever system seems easiest to you.

Some people prefer to use either the temple or the thumb on the side of their wrist as the source of the pulse, and if this is more convenient for you, do it. I sometimes find it difficult to locate my pulse when I use my wrist, so I use my neck.

Playing It Safe: 8 Tips for Water Safety

1. Make sure there's somebody nearby when you swim.

Some instructors will tell you flatly that you should never swim alone, but this can be an impractical rule to follow, especially if you're lucky enough to have your own pool or if you like to swim at odd hours. I swim alone a great deal of the time (although I never swim alone in the ocean), but I like to know there's somebody nearby: not necessarily a lifeguard, but somebody who would be there to give help in the unlikely possibility I run into trouble.

2. Look before you dive.

Diving into water that's too shallow is one of the most dangerous things you can do when you swim, particularly if you do your swimming in a small pool. The water may be deep enough at one end, but it can sometimes get shallow very quickly, and if your dive takes you too far, you could injure yourself severely. I'm very careful about diving. I know that if I ease myself into the water, I'll never get hurt.

3. If you swim, don't drink.

Piña coladas are a nice poolside drink, but go very easy on the alcohol when you're swimming. Alcohol impairs your judgment and can heighten the chances of bumping your head on the side of the pool.

Determining Your Workout Level

As I mentioned earlier, the two variables by which you judge your swimming ability (apart from smoothness and grace) are endurance and speed. There are, of course, any number of ways you can work with these variables. Some swimming instructors maintain that an accomplished swimmer swims at least 4,000

4. Listen to your body.

The minute you sense yourself feeling anything unusual—a chill, a cramp, a feeling of nausea—don't play the hero. Get out of the water as soon as you can.

5. Keep an eye out for other swimmers.

Part of your responsibility as a swimmer is to avoid colliding with other swimmers. At a well-run club, with experienced swimmers, collisions happen rarely. But when you're swimming at a hotel (especially when there are children swimming), you have to be doubly cautious.

6. Know your limits.

The water (and the ocean in particular) is no place to experiment with either your endurance or your courage. Play it safe at all times.

7. Try to keep your wits in an emergency.

This is easier said than done, I know, but most public swimming places are equipped for emergencies. If someone in the water is in trouble, for instance, inform the lifeguard before attempting any lifesaving on your own (unless, of course, you have lifesaving training). And even if you're a strong swimmer, offer a pole, a preserver, or even a towel for the person in trouble to grab on to rather than trying to swim to the person and help him or her back to safety.

yards (about 160 laps in a 25-yard pool) in less than an hour; that is, a hundred yards per minute and twenty seconds, or a 25-yard lap in about twenty seconds. Most YMCA's, on the other hand, maintain that anyone who swims more than 2,000 yards at an average pace of 100 yards per minute and thirty seconds (a 25-yard lap in about twenty-two seconds) is quite good.

The levels I've established for my Hydro-Aerobics workouts

represent a middle ground between these two positions. They can be broken down as follows:

Level I
    Distance: Up to 250 yards without stopping
    Average Speed: 3 minutes or more per 100 yards

Level II
    Distance: Up to 750 yards without stopping
    Average Speed: 2:30 per 100 yards.

Level III
    Distance: Up to 2,500 yards (with brief rest periods allowed) in less than forty minutes
    Average Speed: 1:45 per 100 yards

Level IV
    Distance: 4,000 yards (with brief rest periods) in less than an hour
    Average Speed: 1:20 per 100 yards

Let me make a couple of quick observations about these levels. First, regardless of what level workout you're in, you can derive the full aerobic benefit. Remember, aerobic benefit is a *relative* concept. It's keyed to how hard one's particular cardiovascular system is working when one exercises. That is, a Level I or II swimmer can derive the same aerobic benefit as a Level III or IV swimmer (particularly in the workouts I've set up).

Second, because of the nature of the workouts (notice that even in Level IV, you'll never have to swim more than nine minutes at a stretch), it's important that you swim somewhat *faster* than you would normally swim the longer distance.

The formula I suggest is a very simple one: for every 100 yards *less* than your maximum distance capacity, reduce your time per 100 yards by three seconds. For example, if you swim 1500 yards in forty minutes, 2:06/100 is your pace. If your workout called for swimming eight minutes, you would swim (at your normal rate) one-fifth of your maximum distance, or 300 yards. Since 300 represents twelve 100-yards less than 1500, multiply 12 x 3, which gives you 36. When you subtract thirty-six seconds from 2:06, you get a 1:36/100 pace.

Here's another example. Let's say you're able to swim 2,000 yards at a 1:30/100 pace (this would be about thirty minutes), and your workout calls for only ten minutes of lap swimming. Since ten is one-third of thirty, you would take one-third of 2,000 (666 yards), determine the difference between 2,000 and 666 (1,334) and multiply this difference by three seconds. You end up with about thirty-nine seconds, which gives you the adjusted lap time :51/100.

It's possible that this pace may be too fast for you, in which case you would simply adjust it upward a few seconds until you found a pace that challenged but didn't exhaust you. You may have to do a little experimenting, and you'll have to monitor your pulse rate to make sure you're getting the maximum training effect. After a few workouts, you should be able to find the pace times that suit your needs.

Remember the principle: when you want to increase the aerobic benefit, you don't necessarily have to swim *longer*, only faster.

NOTE ON WORKOUTS: The workouts that follow are pretty much self-explanatory, but there are a few points that bear some clarification.

1. *Lap Swimming*. Lap swimming, unless otherwise indicated, should be freestyle and should be done at your *adjusted* pace, as explained on page 21. It's okay to take an occasional breather during this segment of the workout, but keep the rest periods to less than ten seconds.

2. *Sprints*. Sprints are short bursts of freestyle (or butterfly, if you prefer) in which you swim as fast as you can.

3. *Cool-down*. There are two parts to the cool-down. The first is a *relaxed* swim (about 25 percent slower than your adjusted pace), followed by the stretches. I suggest the sidestroke for your cool-down stroke, but freestyle is fine, too.

LEVEL 1   **General**   *30 Minutes*

1.	The Warm-up (all stretches)	
2.	Bobbing	1 Minute
3.	Laps: Freestyle	1 Minute
4.	Legs, Hips, Thighs, and Buttocks	
	Choose 5 of the following:	
	• The Leg Crossover	5 Reps
	• Front and Back Leg Raise	5 Reps
	• The Side Leg Raise	5 Reps
	• Donkey Kick	5 Reps
	• Thigh Pull	5 Reps
	• The Side Knee Bend	5 Reps
	• The Walking Toe Touch	5 Reps
5.	Bobbing	1 Minute
6.	Laps: Freestyle	Up to 6 minutes
7.	Abdominals	
	Choose 3 of the following:	
	• The Walking Waist Twist	5 Reps
	• The Poolside Sit-up	5 Reps
	• The Sit-up and Thrust	5 Reps
	• The Pike and Stretch	5 Reps
	• The Sidewinder	5 Reps
8.	Bobbing	1 Minute
9.	Laps: Freestyle	Up to 6 minutes
10.	Arms, Shoulders, and Chest	
	Choose 4 of the following:	
	• The Hand Press	5 Reps
	• The Arm Press	5 Reps
	• The Ladder Pull	5 Reps
	• One Arm Ladder Pull	5 Reps
	• The Breaststroke Pull	5 Reps
	• The Arm Cross	5 Reps
	• The Poolside Push-up	5 Reps
11.	Bobbing	1 Minute
12.	Sprint Swim	1 Minute
		(or as much as you can do)
13.	The Cool-down	
	• Any stroke	1 Minute
	• Stretches	1 Minute

LEVEL 1   **Aerobic Emphasis**   *30 Minutes*

1.	The Warm-up (all stretches)	
2.	Bobbing	1 Minute
3.	Laps: Freestyle	3 Minutes
4.	Legs, Hips, Thighs, and Buttocks Choose 4 of the following:	
	• The Leg Crossover	5 Reps
	• Front and Back Leg Raise	5 Reps
	• The Side Leg Raise	5 Reps
	• Donkey Kick	5 Reps
	• Thigh Pull	5 Reps
	• The Side Knee Bend	5 Reps
	• The Walking Toe Touch	5 Reps
5.	Sprint Swim or Kickboard	1 Minute
6.	Bobbing	1 Minute
7.	Laps: any stroke	Up to 6 minutes
8.	Abdominals Choose 4 of the following:	
	• The Walking Waist Twist	5 Reps
	• The Poolside Sit-up	5 Reps
	• The Sit-up and Thrust	5 Reps
	• The Pike and Stretch	5 Reps
	• The Sidewinder	5 Reps
9.	Bobbing	1 Minute
10.	Laps: Freestyle	Up to 6 minutes
11.	Arms, Shoulders, and Chest Choose 4 of the following:	
	• The Hand Press	5 Reps
	• The Arm Press	5 Reps
	• The Ladder Pull	5 Reps
	• One Arm Ladder Pull	5 Reps
	• The Breaststroke Pull	5 Reps
	• The Arm Cross	5 Reps
	• The Poolside Push-up	5 Reps
12.	Sprint Swim or Kickboard	1 Minute
13.	Laps: Freestyle	5 Minutes
14.	The Cool-down	
	• Any stroke	1 Minute
	• Stretches	1 Minute

LEVEL 1 **Flexibility Emphasis** *30 Minutes*

1.	The Warm-up (all stretches)	
2.	Bobbing	1 Minute
3.	Laps: Freestyle	3 Minutes
4.	Legs, Hips, Thighs, and Buttocks	
	Choose 5 of the following:	
	• The Leg Crossover	7 Reps
	• Front and Back Leg Raise	7 Reps
	• The Side Leg Raise	7 Reps
	• Donkey Kick	7 Reps
	• Thigh Pull	7 Reps
	• The Side Knee Bend	7 Reps
	• The Walking Toe Touch	7 Reps
5.	Bobbing	1 Minute
6.	Laps: Freestyle	Up to 6 minutes
7.	Abdominals	
	Choose 4 of the following:	
	• The Walking Waist Twist	7 Reps
	• The Poolside Sit-up	7 Reps
	• The Sit-up and Thrust	7 Reps
	• The Pike and Stretch	7 Reps
	• The Sidewinder	7 Reps
8.	Bobbing	1 Minute
9.	Laps: Freestyle	Up to 6 minutes
10.	Arms, Shoulders, and Chest	
	Choose 4 of the following:	
	• The Hand Press	7 Reps
	• The Arm Press	7 Reps
	• The Ladder Pull	7 Reps
	• One Arm Ladder Pull	7 Reps
	• The Breaststroke Pull	7 Reps
	• The Arm Cross	7 Reps
	• The Poolside Push-up	7 Reps
11.	Bobbing	1 Minute
12.	Laps: Breaststroke (Option: Freestyle)	5 Minutes
13.	The Cool-down	
	• Any stroke	1 Minute
	• Stretches	1 Minute

LEVEL 1 **Strength Emphasis** *30 Minutes*

1.	The Warm-up (all stretches)	
2.	Laps: Freestyle	3 Minutes
3.	Legs, Hips, Thighs, and Buttocks	
	Choose 4 of the following:	
	• The Leg Crossover	6 Reps
	• Front and Back Leg Raise	6 Reps
	• The Side Leg Raise	6 Reps
	• Donkey Kick	6 Reps
	• Thigh Pull	6 Reps
	• The Side Knee Bend	6 Reps
	• The Walking Toe Touch	6 Reps
4.	Bobbing	1 Minute
5.	Kickboard	2 Minutes
6.	Laps: Freestyle	Up to 6 minutes
7.	Abdominals	
	Do all of the following:	
	• The Walking Waist Twist	6 Reps
	• The Poolside Sit-up	6 Reps
	• The Sit-up and Thrust	6 Reps
	• The Pike and Stretch	6 Reps
	• The Sidewinder	6 Reps
8.	Bobbing	1 Minute
9.	Laps: Freestyle	Up to 6 minutes
10.	Arms, Shoulders, and Chest	
	Choose 6 of the following:	
	• The Hand Press	7 Reps
	• The Arm Press	7 Reps
	• The Ladder Pull	7 Reps
	• One Arm Ladder Pull	7 Reps
	• The Breaststroke Pull	7 Reps
	• The Arm Cross	7 Reps
	• The Poolside Push-up	7 Reps
11.	Kickboard	1 Minute
12.	Bobbing	1 Minute
13.	Laps: Freestyle	5 Minutes
14.	The Cool-down	
	• Any stroke	1 Minute
	• Stretches	1 Minute

LEVEL II   **General**   *35 Minutes*

1.	The Warm-up (all stretches)	
2.	Bobbing	1 Minute
3.	Laps: Freestyle	3 Minutes
4.	Legs, Hips, Thighs, and Buttocks	
	Choose 5 of the following:	
	• The Leg Crossover	7 Reps
	• Front and Back Leg Raise	7 Reps
	• The Side Leg Raise	7 Reps
	• Donkey Kick	7 Reps
	• Thigh Pull	7 Reps
	• The Side Knee Bend	7 Reps
	• The Walking Toe Touch	7 Reps
5.	Bobbing	1 Minute
6.	Laps: Freestyle	7 Minutes
7.	Abdominals	
	Choose 3 of the following:	
	• The Walking Waist Twist	7 Reps
	• The Poolside Sit-up	7 Reps
	• The Sit-up and Thrust	7 Reps
	• The Pike and Stretch	7 Reps
	• The Sidewinder	7 Reps
8.	Bobbing	1 Minute
9.	Laps: any stroke	7 Minutes
10.	Arms, Shoulders, and Chest	
	Choose 4 of the following:	
	• The Hand Press	6 Reps
	• The Arm Press	6 Reps
	• The Ladder Pull	6 Reps
	• One Arm Ladder Pull	6 Reps
	• The Breaststroke Pull	6 Reps
	• The Arm Cross	6 Reps
	• The Poolside Push-up	6 Reps
11.	Bobbing	1 Minute
12.	Sprint Swim	1 Minute
13.	Laps: Freestyle	5 Minutes
14.	The Cool-down	
	• Any stroke	1½ Minutes
	• Stretches	1 Minute

LEVEL II **Aerobic Emphasis** *35 Minutes*

1.	The Warm-up (all stretches)	
2.	Bobbing	1 Minute
3.	Laps: Freestyle	3 Minutes
4.	Legs, Hips, Thighs, and Buttocks	
	Choose 5 of the following:	
	• The Leg Crossover	7 Reps
	• Front and Back Leg Raise	7 Reps
	• The Side Leg Raise	7 Reps
	• Donkey Kick	7 Reps
	• Thigh Pull	7 Reps
	• The Side Knee Bend	7 Reps
	• The Walking Toe Touch	7 Reps
5.	Sprint Swim	1 Minute
6.	Bobbing	1 Minute
7.	Laps: Freestyle	7 Minutes
8.	Abdominals	
	Do all of the following:	
	• The Walking Waist Twist	7 Reps
	• The Poolside Sit-up	7 Reps
	• The Sit-up and Thrust	7 Reps
	• The Pike and Stretch	7 Reps
	• The Sidewinder	7 Reps
9.	Bobbing	1 Minute
10.	Laps: any stroke	7 Minutes
11.	Arms, Shoulders, and Chest	
	Choose 5 of the following:	
	• The Hand Press	7 Reps
	• The Arm Press	7 Reps
	• The Ladder Pull	7 Reps
	• One Arm Ladder Pull	7 Reps
	• The Breaststroke Pull	7 Reps
	• The Arm Cross	7 Reps
	• The Poolside Push-up	7 Reps
12.	Sprint Swim or Kickboard	1 Minute
13.	Laps: Freestyle	3 Minutes
14.	The Cool-down	
	• Any stroke	1 Minute
	• Stretches	1 Minute

LEVEL II **Flexibility Emphasis** *35 Minutes*

1.	The Warm-up (all stretches)	
2.	Bobbing	1 Minute
3.	Laps: Freestyle	3 Minutes
4.	Legs, Hips, Thighs, and Buttocks	
	Choose 6 of the following:	
	• The Leg Crossover	8 Reps
	• Front and Back Leg Raise	8 Reps
	• The Side Leg Raise	8 Reps
	• Donkey Kick	8 Reps
	• Thigh Pull	8 Reps
	• The Side Knee Bend	8 Reps
	• The Walking Toe Touch	8 Reps
5.	Bobbing	1 Minute
6.	Laps: Freestyle	7 Minutes
7.	Abdominals	
	Do all of the following:	
	• The Walking Waist Twist	8 Reps
	• The Poolside Sit-up	8 Reps
	• The Sit-up and Thrust	8 Reps
	• The Pike and Stretch	8 Reps
	• The Sidewinder	8 Reps
8.	Bobbing	1 Minute
9.	Laps: Freestyle	7 Minutes
10.	Arms, Shoulders, and Chest	
	Choose 5 of the following:	
	• The Hand Press	8 Reps
	• The Arm Press	8 Reps
	• The Ladder Pull	8 Reps
	• One Arm Ladder Pull	8 Reps
	• The Breaststroke Pull	8 Reps
	• The Arm Cross	8 Reps
	• The Poolside Push-up	8 Reps
11.	Bobbing	1 Minute
12.	Laps: Breaststroke (Option: Freestyle)	4 Minutes
13.	Bobbing	1 Minute
14.	The Cool-down	
	• Any stroke	1½ Minutes
	• Stretches	1 Minute

LEVEL II **Strength Emphasis** *35 Minutes*

1.	The Warm-up (all stretches)	
2.	Laps: Freestyle	3 Minutes
3.	Legs, Hips, Thighs, and Buttocks	
	Choose 5 of the following:	
	• The Leg Crossover	7 Reps
	• Front and Back Leg Raise	7 Reps
	• The Side Leg Raise	7 Reps
	• Donkey Kick	7 Reps
	• Thigh Pull	7 Reps
	• The Side Knee Bend	7 Reps
	• The Walking Toe Touch	7 Reps
4.	Bobbing	1 Minute
5.	Kickboard	2 Minutes
6.	Laps: Freestyle	7 Minutes
7.	Abdominals	
	Do all of the following:	
	• The Walking Waist Twist	8 Reps
	• The Poolside Sit-up	8 Reps
	• The Sit-up and Thrust	8 Reps
	• The Pike and Stretch	8 Reps
	• The Sidewinder	8 Reps
8.	Bobbing	1 Minute
9.	Laps: any stroke	7 Minutes
10.	Arms, Shoulders, and Chest	
	Do all of the following:	
	• The Hand Press	8 Reps
	• The Arm Press	8 Reps
	• The Ladder Pull	8 Reps
	• One Arm Ladder Pull	8 Reps
	• The Breaststroke Pull	8 Reps
	• The Arm Cross	8 Reps
	• The Poolside Push-up	8 Reps
11.	Kickboard	2 Minutes
12.	Bobbing	1 Minute
13.	Laps: Freestyle	6 Minutes
14.	The Cool-down	
	• Any stroke	1½ Minutes
	• Stretches	1 Minute

LEVEL III General *40 Minutes*

1.	The Warm-up (all stretches)	
2.	Bobbing	1 Minute
3.	Laps: Freestyle	3 Minutes
4.	Legs, Hips, Thighs, and Buttocks	
	Choose 6 of the following:	
	• The Leg Crossover	8 Reps
	• Front and Back Leg Raise	8 Reps
	• The Side Leg Raise	8 Reps
	• Donkey Kick	8 Reps
	• Thigh Pull	8 Reps
	• The Side Knee Bend	8 Reps
	• The Walking Toe Touch	8 Reps
5.	Bobbing	1 Minute
6.	Laps: Freestyle	8 Minutes
7.	Abdominals	
	Choose 4 of the following:	
	• The Walking Waist Twist	8 Reps
	• The Poolside Sit-up	8 Reps
	• The Sit-up and Thrust	8 Reps
	• The Pike and Stretch	8 Reps
	• The Sidewinder	8 Reps
8.	Bobbing	1 Minute
9.	Laps: any stroke	8 Minutes
10.	Arms, Shoulders, and Chest	
	Choose 5 of the following:	
	• The Hand Press	8 Reps
	• The Arm Press	8 Reps
	• The Ladder Pull	8 Reps
	• One Arm Ladder Pull	8 Reps
	• The Breaststroke Pull	8 Reps
	• The Arm Cross	8 Reps
	• The Poolside Push-up	8 Reps
11.	Bobbing	1 Minute
12.	Sprint Swim	1 Minute
13.	Bobbing	1 Minute
14.	Laps: Freestyle	7 Minutes
15.	The Cool-down	
	• Any stroke	2 Minutes
	• Stretches	1 Minute

LEVEL III **Aerobic Emphasis** *40 Minutes*

1.	The Warm-up (all stretches)	
2.	Bobbing	1 Minute
3.	Laps: Freestyle	3 Minutes
4.	Legs, Hips, Thighs, and Buttocks	
	Choose 5 of the following:	
	• The Leg Crossover	8 Reps
	• Front and Back Leg Raise	8 Reps
	• The Side Leg Raise	8 Reps
	• Donkey Kick	8 Reps
	• Thigh Pull	8 Reps
	• The Side Knee Bend	8 Reps
	• The Walking Toe Touch	8 Reps
5.	Sprint Swim	1 Minute
6.	Bobbing	1 Minute
7.	Laps: Freestyle	8 Minutes
8.	Abdominals	
	Do all of the following:	
	• The Walking Waist Twist	8 Reps
	• The Poolside Sit-up	8 Reps
	• The Sit-up and Thrust	8 Reps
	• The Pike and Stretch	8 Reps
	• The Sidewinder	8 Reps
9.	Bobbing	1 Minute
10.	Laps: Freestyle	8 Minutes
11.	Arms, Shoulders, and Chest	
	Choose 6 of the following:	
	• The Hand Press	8 Reps
	• The Arm Press	8 Reps
	• The Ladder Pull	8 Reps
	• One Arm Ladder Pull	8 Reps
	• The Breaststroke Pull	8 Reps
	• The Arm Cross	8 Reps
	• The Poolside Push-up	8 Reps
12.	Sprint Swim	1 Minute
13.	Laps: Freestyle	7 Minutes
14.	The Cool-down	
	• Any stroke	2 Minutes
	• Stretches	1 Minute

LEVEL III **Flexibility Emphasis** *40 Minutes*

1.	The Warm-up (all stretches)	
2.	Bobbing	1 Minute
3.	Laps: Freestyle	3 Minutes
4.	Legs, Hips, Thighs, and Buttocks	
	Choose 6 of the following:	
	• The Leg Crossover	9 Reps
	• Front and Back Leg Raise	9 Reps
	• The Side Leg Raise	9 Reps
	• Donkey Kick	9 Reps
	• Thigh Pull	9 Reps
	• The Side Knee Bend	9 Reps
	• The Walking Toe Touch	9 Reps
5.	Bobbing	1 Minute
6.	Laps: Freestyle	8 Minutes
7.	Abdominals	
	Do all of the following:	
	• The Walking Waist Twist	9 Reps
	• The Poolside Sit-up	9 Reps
	• The Sit-up and Thrust	9 Reps
	• The Pike and Stretch	9 Reps
	• The Sidewinder	9 Reps
8.	Bobbing	1 Minute
9.	Laps: Freestyle	8 Minutes
10.	Arms, Shoulders, and Chest	
	Choose 5 of the following:	
	• The Hand Press	9 Reps
	• The Arm Press	9 Reps
	• The Ladder Pull	9 Reps
	• One Arm Ladder Pull	9 Reps
	• The Breaststroke Pull	9 Reps
	• The Arm Cross	9 Reps
	• The Poolside Push-up	9 Reps
11.	Bobbing	1 Minute
12.	Laps: Breaststroke (Option: Freestyle)	4 Minutes
13.	The Cool-down	
	• Any stroke	2 Minutes
	• Stretches	1 Minute

LEVEL III **Strength Emphasis** *40 Minutes*

1.	The Warm-up (all stretches)	
2.	Laps: Freestyle	3 Minutes
3.	Legs, Hips, Thighs, and Buttocks	
	Choose 6 of the following:	
	• The Leg Crossover	8 Reps
	• Front and Back Leg Raise	8 Reps
	• The Side Leg Raise	8 Reps
	• Donkey Kick	8 Reps
	• Thigh Pull	8 Reps
	• The Side Knee Bend	8 Reps
	• The Walking Toe Touch	8 Reps
4.	Bobbing	1 Minute
5.	Kickboard	2 Minutes
6.	Laps: Freestyle	7 Minutes
7.	Abdominals	
	Do all of the following:	
	• The Walking Waist Twist	8 Reps
	• The Poolside Sit-up	8 Reps
	• The Sit-up and Thrust	8 Reps
	• The Pike and Stretch	8 Reps
	• The Sidewinder	8 Reps
8.	Bobbing	1 Minute
9.	Laps: any stroke	7 Minutes
10.	Arms, Shoulders, and Chest	
	Do all of the following:	
	• The Hand Press	8 Reps
	• The Arm Press	8 Reps
	• The Ladder Pull	8 Reps
	• One Arm Ladder Pull	8 Reps
	• The Breaststroke Pull	8 Reps
	• The Arm Cross	8 Reps
	• The Poolside Push-up	8 Reps
11.	Kickboard	1 Minute
12.	Bobbing	1 Minute
13.	Laps: Freestyle	7 Minutes
14.	The Cool-down	
	• Any stroke	2 Minutes
	• Stretches	1 Minute

LEVEL IV   **General**   *45 Minutes*

1.	The Warm-up (all stretches)	
2.	Bobbing	1 Minute
3.	Laps: Freestyle	3 Minutes
4.	Legs, Hips, Thighs, and Buttocks	
	Choose 6 of the following:	
	• The Leg Crossover	10 Reps
	• Front and Back Leg Raise	10 Reps
	• The Side Leg Raise	10 Reps
	• Donkey Kick	10 Reps
	• Thigh Pull	10 Reps
	• The Side Knee Bend	10 Reps
	• The Walking Toe Touch	10 Reps
5.	Bobbing	1 Minute
6.	Laps: Freestyle	9 Minutes
7.	Bobbing	1 Minute
8.	Abdominals	
	Choose 4 of the following:	
	• The Walking Waist Twist	10 Reps
	• The Poolside Sit-up	10 Reps
	• The Sit-up and Thrust	10 Reps
	• The Pike and Stretch	10 Reps
	• The Sidewinder	10 Reps
9.	Bobbing	1 Minute
10.	Laps: Freestyle	9 Minutes
11.	Arms, Shoulders, and Chest	
	Choose 4 of the following:	
	• The Hand Press	8 Reps
	• The Arm Press	8 Reps
	• The Ladder Pull	8 Reps
	• One Arm Ladder Pull	8 Reps
	• The Breaststroke Pull	8 Reps
	• The Arm Cross	8 Reps
	• The Poolside Push-up	8 Reps
12.	Spring Swim	1 Minute
13.	Bobbing	1 Minute
14.	Laps: Freestyle	8 Minutes
15.	The Cool-down	
	• Any stroke	2½ Minutes
	• Stretches	1 Minute

LEVEL IV **Aerobic Emphasis** *45 Minutes*

1.	The Warm-up (all stretches)	
2.	Bobbing	1 Minute
3.	Laps: Freestyle	3 Minutes
4.	Legs, Hips, Thighs, and Buttocks	
	Choose 5 of the following:	
	• The Leg Crossover	10 Reps
	• Front and Back Leg Raise	10 Reps
	• The Side Leg Raise	10 Reps
	• Donkey Kick	10 Reps
	• Thigh Pull	10 Reps
	• The Side Knee Bend	10 Reps
	• The Walking Toe Touch	10 Reps
5.	Bobbing	1 Minute
6.	Laps: Freestyle	9 Minutes
7.	Abdominals	
	Do all of the following:	
	• The Walking Waist Twist	10 Reps
	• The Poolside Sit-up	10 Reps
	• The Sit-up and Thrust	10 Reps
	• The Pike and Stretch	10 Reps
	• The Sidewinder	10 Reps
8.	Bobbing	1 Minute
9.	Laps: Freestyle	9 Minutes
10.	Arms, Shoulders, and Chest	
	Choose 5 of the following:	
	• The Hand Press	8 Reps
	• The Arm Press	8 Reps
	• The Ladder Pull	8 Reps
	• One Arm Ladder Pull	8 Reps
	• The Breaststroke Pull	8 Reps
	• The Arm Cross	8 Reps
	• The Poolside Push-up	8 Reps
11.	Spring Swim	1 Minute
12.	Bobbing	1 Minute
13.	Laps: any stroke	7 Minutes
14.	The Cool-down	
	• Any stroke	2½ Minutes
	• Stretches	1 Minute

LEVEL IV **Flexibility Emphasis** *45 Minutes*

1.	The Warm-up (all stretches)	
2.	Bobbing	1 Minute
3.	Laps: Freestyle	3 Minutes
4.	Legs, Hips, Thighs, and Buttocks	
	Do all of the following:	
	• The Leg Crossover	10 Reps
	• Front and Back Leg Raise	10 Reps
	• The Side Leg Raise	10 Reps
	• Donkey Kick	10 Reps
	• Thigh Pull	10 Reps
	• The Side Knee Bend	10 Reps
	• The Walking Toe Touch	10 Reps
5.	Laps: Freestyle	9 Minutes
6.	Abdominals	
	Do all of the following:	
	• The Walking Waist Twist	10 Reps
	• The Poolside Sit-up	10 Reps
	• The Sit-up and Thrust	10 Reps
	• The Pike and Stretch	10 Reps
	• The Sidewinder	10 Reps
7.	Sprint Swim	1 Minute
8.	Laps: Freestyle	9 Minutes
9.	Arms, Shoulders, and Chest	
	Choose 6 of the following:	
	• The Hand Press	10 Reps
	• The Arm Press	10 Reps
	• The Ladder Pull	10 Reps
	• One Arm Ladder Pull	10 Reps
	• The Breaststroke Pull	10 Reps
	• The Arm Cross	10 Reps
	• The Poolside Push-up	10 Reps
10.	Sprint Swim	1 Minute
11.	Laps: Breaststroke (Option: Freestyle)	3 Minutes
12.	The Cool-down	
	• Any stroke	2½ Minutes
	• Stretches	1 Minute

LEVEL IV **Strength Emphasis** *45 Minutes*

1.	The Warm-up (all stretches)	
2.	Laps: Freestyle	3 Minutes
3.	Legs, Hips, Thighs, and Buttocks	
	Do all of the following:	
	• The Leg Crossover	8 Reps
	• Front and Back Leg Raise	8 Reps
	• The Side Leg Raise	8 Reps
	• Donkey Kick	8 Reps
	• Thigh Pull	8 Reps
	• The Side Knee Bend	8 Reps
	• The Walking Toe Touch	8 Reps
4.	Kickboard	3 Minutes
5.	Bobbing	1 Minute
6.	Laps: Freestyle	9 Minutes
7.	Abdominals	
	Do all of the following:	
	• The Walking Waist Twist	10 Reps
	• The Poolside Sit-up	10 Reps
	• The Sit-up and Thrust	10 Reps
	• The Pike and Stretch	10 Reps
	• The Sidewinder	10 Reps
8.	Sprint Swim	1 Minute
9.	Bobbing	1 Minute
10.	Laps: any stroke	9 Minutes
11.	Arms, Shoulders, and Chest	
	Do all of the following:	
	• The Hand Press	10 Reps
	• The Arm Press	10 Reps
	• The Ladder Pull	10 Reps
	• One Arm Ladder Pull	10 Reps
	• The Breaststroke Pull	10 Reps
	• The Arm Cross	10 Reps
	• The Poolside Push-up	10 Reps
12.	Kickboard	2 Minutes
13.	Laps: Freestyle	6 Minutes
14.	The Cool-down	
	• Any stroke	2½ Minutes
	• Stretches	1 Minute

8· THE HYDRO-AEROBICS LIFE-STYLE

I would never have become an Olympic swimmer if my older brother hadn't injured his knee.

My older brother (like my father and, for that matter, like my younger brother and younger sister) was a great athlete whose first love was baseball. I was one of those younger sisters who wanted to be just like her older brother, so my first love was baseball, too. In fact, when I was nine years old, I spent an entire summer doing nothing but going to every one of my brother's baseball games. I never got a chance to play, of course, but I did get a chance to wear the team uniform, and I couldn't have been more thrilled about it. A feminist I wasn't.

Then came my brother's knee injury—an injury that made it difficult for him to play competitive ball. So what he did was take up competitive swimming instead, and I followed suit. The difference, though, was that as a swimmer, I didn't have to be a cheerleader. I could compete with myself.

I wasn't "born" to be an Olympic swimmer. True, I was exposed to the water early (I was born in San Diego and my father used to take me to Mission Beach whenever he could), and I was swimming when I was three years old. But I didn't start swimming seriously until I was about ten years old—which is very late for a swimmer—and at that, I began as the slowest swimmer on my first team.

Getting better wasn't easy, and I sometimes wonder why I didn't become discouraged at the beginning. In retrospect, the reason is that I genuinely loved the life; not just the competition but the practices, the people, the camaraderie, the travel. I enjoyed simply being *near* a swimming pool—so much so that I spent the summers of my early adolescence selling candy and towels in the locker room of a swim club so that I could swim there and compete against the boy swimmers.

The competition aspect of swimming was probably what I liked *least* about it. So my decision to quit competitive swimming at the age of seventeen, a few months after I'd won my two Olympic gold medals, wasn't as tough for me as some people may have thought. I wasn't giving up *swimming*. I was simply giving up the kind of pressure that I had never really enjoyed in the first place.

Still it wasn't an easy transition. For one thing, I had to adjust to a world that was not nearly as predictable, as nurturing, or as simple as the one I'd lived in as a competitive swimmer. For another, I had to change some basic life-style habits, not the least of which was my eating habits. (While I was competing, I used to swim an average of 7000 meters a day, which can burn an awful lot of calories.)

But I made the transition, and I like to think that swimming had a lot to do with it. Swimming, as I mentioned in the Introduction, is more than just a fitness activity for me; it has always been my centering device, my way of staying in tune with who I am, my way of developing the perspective that I find so essential in order to survive, let alone succeed, in today's world. And if I have accomplished anything in this book, I would hope that I have convinced you that you can use swimming in general and Hydro-Aerobics in particular to make a truly meaningful difference in your life.

Not that it will necessarily be that easy for you. Simply finding the three hours or so to work out each week could be a problem. You may have a job that drains most of your time and energy, and you may have a young family that puts constant demands on your time. If this is the case, all I can say is that no matter how busy you are, you can *find* the time, as long as you attach enough importance to your health and your well-being. The question I would ask, in fact, is whether you can afford *not* to spend these few hours doing something that's going to make you better at your job or better able to handle your family.

The thing you have to keep reminding yourself over and over again is that fitness isn't a luxury; neither is it something that's important only if you compete in athletics. Fitness is the very cornerstone of a satisfying life, regardless of who you are and what you do. Fitness (or the lack of it) affects everything you do, from how you feel when you first open your eyes in the morning to how you feel when you go to sleep at night. It affects the way you eat, sleep, work, and play. It affects your appearance, your moods, and your relationships.

And there is no mystery to fitness—not anymore, anyway. We know that if you exercise your cardiovascular system for long enough periods each week, your stamina will improve; that if you do stretching and calisthenics, your flexibility will improve; and if you do resistance exercises, your strength will increase. There's only one catch: You have to do the workouts, whether you do them on a running track, in a gym, or, in the case of Hydro-Aerobics, in the water.

The choice lies with you. Contrary to what many people will tell you, getting involved in a regular fitness program isn't so much a matter of self-discipline. It's more a matter of deciding, once and for all, that you *deserve* the benefits of fitness. And once you make that decision, the rest takes care of itself.

Some Basic Fitness Guidelines

I don't consider myself an expert on health and fitness, but I know what has worked for me throughout my life, and so I'd like to share a few basic ideas with you.

1. Do stretches first thing in the morning.

Get into the habit of starting each morning with four or five basic body stretches (you can use the same stretches I described in the warm-up section of the workouts). Do them slowly and pay attention to your body as you're doing them. Stretching the first thing in the morning not only stimulates your circulation, it helps put you in a relaxed state of mind.

2. Eat and drink sensibly.

A sensible diet is built around two basic principles: moderation and variety. I don't deny myself many foods, but I don't binge or overindulge. I try to limit sweets (I eat fresh fruit instead), and I tend to eat more poultry and fish than I do beef. I also try my best to eat three fairly balanced meals rather than skipping a meal so that I won't be ravenous by the time the next meal comes around. And I try to be as moderate as I can when it comes to alcohol. I generally like to have a glass of wine with dinner (especially if I'm on the road), but if I drink any more I can feel it the next morning.

3. Drink plenty of water.

Whether you exercise or not, you need at least six glasses of water a day to keep your body running efficiently, and you should make it a point to drink this amount whether you're thirsty or not. If you're not sure of the quality of the water you drink, spend a few dollars a month on bottled water.

4. Pay attention to your posture.

Your posture not only affects the way you look, it can mean the difference between a back that's healthy or chronically aching. I first learned about good posture when I began taking ballet lessons, and I've always been grateful. I learned to stand with my head upright and thrown slightly back, my shoulders comfortably back (in between the military posture and the familiar slump), and my stomach pulled in just a little. I also learned how to sit properly, with my spine straight.

5. Get the right amount of sleep.

I know people who can get along with as few as four or five hours of sleep a night, but I'm not one of them. I happen to need eight hours. Otherwise I simply don't feel as energetic as I'd like to the next day. The important thing is to discover for yourself what the optimum number of hours of sleep is for you and do your best to get the amount as regularly as you can.

6. Minimize the effects of stress.

It's next to impossible to avoid stress in today's world, but there are any number of things you can do to minimize the damage that stress can do to your body. I've discovered, for instance, that no matter how much stress I have to deal with on any given day, I always feel better at the end of the day if sometime in the middle of it I can manage to get in a 30-minute workout. I know people who do a set of deep-breathing exercises several times a day, and I have a friend who keeps a timer on his desk and sets it so that he never works for more than 45 minutes straight. He will then take at least a 10- or 15-minute break, at which time he'll do some stretches or take a short walk. He insists he's twice as productive as he used to be and is not nearly as tired at the end of the day.

Make the decision. And let Hydro-Aerobics be the vehicle that carries you through the decision. By now you should be well aware of the benefits of the program: its variety, its safety, its convenience, and its ability to work as a basic fitness activity not only for today and tomorrow, but for years and years to come. All that remains now is for you to incorporate the program into your life-style. Believe me, it won't be hard to do—the program will start paying benefits as soon as you begin; and the more you do the workouts, the more you'll come to enjoy and look forward to them.

About the Authors

Donna de Varona broke eighteen world records in addition to winning two Olympic gold medals during her illustrious career as a swimmer. She is currently an announcer for ABC sports and a member of the U.S. Olympic Committee. She served as a consultant to the 1984 Olympic Games.

Donna de Varona helped create the concept of the Special Olympics program in 1969. She is a founding member and most recently president of the Women's Sports Foundation, and serves on the President's Council on Physical Fitness.

Barry Tarshis has written or co-authored more than twenty books including the bestselling *The Robert Half Way To Getting Hired in Today's Market*.